TWILIGHT
THE COMPLETE JOURNEY

Entertainment WEEKLY

TWILIGHT
THE COMPLETE JOURNEY
FROM THE EDITORS OF ENTERTAINMENT WEEKLY

EDITORS **Jeff Giles, Missy Schwartz** | ART DIRECTOR **Tracy Toscano**
DESIGNER **Jorge Colombo** | PHOTO EDITOR **Rosanna Sguera**

EDIT PRODUCTION **Rachel Orvino** | ASSOCIATE EDITOR **Toni Rumore**
REPORTER **V.R. Peterson** | COPY EDITORS **Dan Morrissey, Ben Spier**

ADDITIONAL CONTRIBUTORS
**Kelly Borgeson, Helen Eisenbach, Nolan Feeney,
Adrienne Onofri, Andrew Santana, Marc Snetiker**

SPECIAL THANKS
**Eric Kops, Louise Kaufman, Clarissa Colmenero,
Nancy Kirkpatrick, Elizabeth Eulberg, Freyda Tavin**

TIME HOME ENTERTAINMENT INC.
EDITORIAL DIRECTOR **Stephen Koepp**
EDITORIAL OPERATIONS DIRECTOR **Michael Q. Bullerdick**

PUBLISHER **Jim Childs**
VICE PRESIDENT, BUSINESS DEVELOPMENT & STRATEGY **Steven Sandonato**
EXECUTIVE DIRECTOR, MARKETING SERVICES **Carol Pittard**
EXECUTIVE DIRECTOR, RETAIL & SPECIAL SALES **Tom Mifsud**
EXECUTIVE PUBLISHING DIRECTOR **Joy Butts**
DIRECTOR, BOOKAZINE DEVELOPMENT & MARKETING **Laura Adam**
FINANCE DIRECTOR **Glenn Buonocore**
ASSOCIATE PUBLISHING DIRECTOR **Megan Pearlman**
ASSISTANT GENERAL COUNSEL **Helen Wan**
ASSISTANT DIRECTOR, SPECIAL SALES **Ilene Schreider**
SENIOR BOOK PRODUCTION MANAGER **Susan Chodakiewicz**
DESIGN & PREPRESS MANAGER **Anne-Michelle Gallero**
BRAND ASSISTANT MANAGER **Hillary Hirsch**
ASSOCIATE PREPRESS MANAGER **Alex Voznesenskiy**

SPECIAL THANKS
**Christine Austin, Jeremy Biloon, Rose Cirrincione, Lauren Hall Clark,
Jacqueline Fitzgerald, Christine Font, Jenna Goldberg, Suzanne Janso, David Kahn,
Mona Li, Amy Mangus, Robert Marasco, Kimberly Marshall, Amy Migliaccio,
Nina Mistry, Dave Rozzelle, Adriana Tierno, Vanessa Wu**

Edward and Bella

CONTENTS

COVER PHOTOGRAPHED FOR EW BY SAM JONES ON NOV. 4, 2011, IN LOS ANGELES

Robert Pattinson
and Kristen Stewart
photographed for EW by
James White on Sept. 16,
2008, in Los Angeles

FOREWORD

ENTERTAINMENT WEEKLY STARTED WRITING ABOUT *The Twilight Saga* long before the other big magazines woke up and discovered a phenomenon already in progress. One great upside was that EW won the trust of Stephenie Meyer and the cast. Even when they started to dread doing press, they baked our writers pies, hugged them at Comic-Con, and talked to them honestly (and often hilariously) about their lives, fears, and careers. As you'll see in this book, they also gave our photographers extraordinary shots that will look awesome on your wall.

ENTERTAINMENT WEEKLY's *Twilight: The Complete Journey* represents the best of five years' worth of behind-the-scenes access. The book tells the story precisely as it happened. So you'll meet the stars when they're still unknowns: Robert Pattinson will be a funny, neurotic 22-year-old who keeps asking Kristen Stewart to marry him even though she has a boyfriend. Stewart will be a smart, searching, and willful 17-year-old who insists on changing dialogue she thinks is cheesy. And Taylor Lautner will hit the ground running at a supernaturally sweet 16, shocked that his name is already being stitched into women's underwear. Then you'll see what changes when fame arrives—and what doesn't.

As Pattinson told us in the first real interview he ever gave, actors tend to be coached to say as little as possible. But what if they're actually proud of being raw and real? Turns out you can learn a lot about how Hollywood works from three young stars who want to tell the truth.

Jeff Giles
Deputy Managing Editor
ENTERTAINMENT WEEKLY

Stewart and Taylor
Lautner photographed
for EW by Ben Watts
on June 3, 2009,
in Agoura, Calif.

Pattinson and Stewart
photographed for EW
by Jeff Riedel
on June 6, 2008,
in Los Angeles

Stewart and
Pattinson
photographed for
EW by James White
on Sept. 16, 2008,
in Los Angeles

Pattinson, Stewart, and
Lautner photographed
for EW by Sam Jones
on Nov. 4, 2011,
in Los Angeles

Stephenie Meyer
photographed for
EW by Eric Ogden
on May 21, 2008,
in Los Angeles

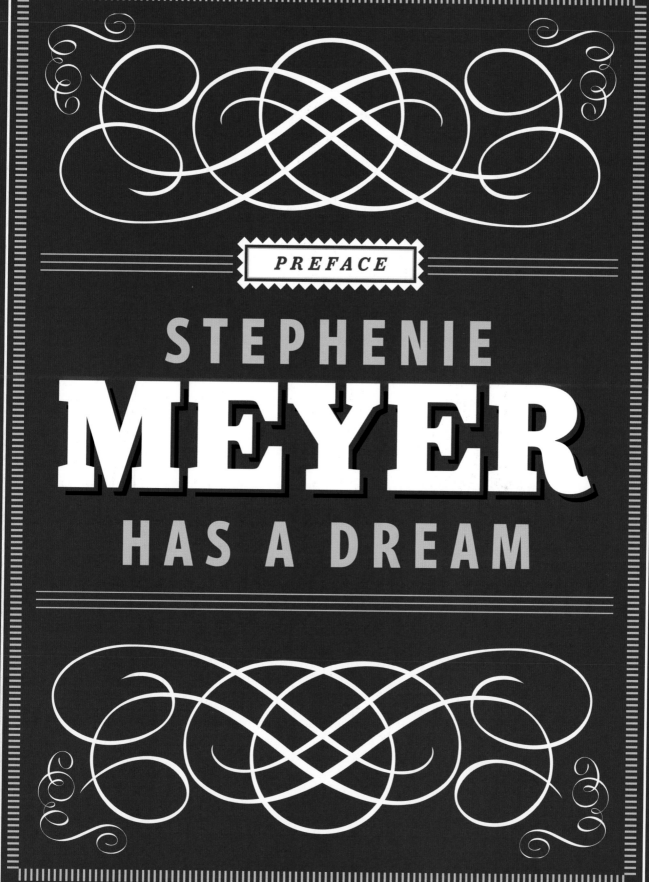

STEPHENIE MEYER HAS A DREAM

THE
STORYTELLER

*We first met **Stephenie Meyer** in 2008.
Her Twilight novels were already best-sellers, but Hollywood
was about to take her empire to a whole new level.*

BY **KAREN VALBY**

O **N A JUNE NIGHT IN 2003,** Stephenie Meyer dreamed of a girl meeting up with a vampire in the woods. The next morning, she got up, started writing for what was essentially the first time in her life, and just three months later finished a 500-page book about a 17-year-old named Bella and her gorgeous god of a vampire boyfriend, Edward. Mystified as to how a nice housewife living in Phoenix goes about cracking the New York publishing world, Meyer joined a cozy writers' group of supportive women working on trivia books, Hallmark cards, and song lyrics. On a lark, she got up the nerve to contact a handful of literary agents whose names she'd found online, sending them each a tease about *Twilight*. The right one bit, and landed her new client a three-book deal for $750,000. ("I'd been hoping for $10,000 to pay off my minivan," says Meyer.) Uncertain what to expect from their new Mormon author, Little, Brown Books for Young Readers later dispatched a publicist to Arizona—to make sure, as Meyer says with a laugh, "I wasn't wearing a skirt over my jeans or something."

Today, Meyer, 34, is a *New York Times* best-seller, a published author in nearly 50 countries, a millionaire many times over, and, according to fans and booksellers alike, the second coming of J.K. Rowling. When *Eclipse*, the third installment in the *Twilight Saga*, came out last summer, it shook hands with Harry Potter before sweetly knocking him from his perch at No. 1. On Aug. 2, 2008, at 12:01 a.m., cash registers everywhere will start ringing with sales of *Breaking Dawn*, Meyer's feverishly anticipated fourth and final volume. The fervor won't die down then, either, as fans can direct their passionate gaze toward the December release of the *Twilight* movie.

One day in May 2008, Meyer is in Salt Lake City promoting her first adult novel, *The Host*, a vigorous blend of romance and science fiction that sold at auction for $600,000 and debuted at No. 1. In the audience, a thousand restless fans scream for the author at a decibel level normally reserved for boy bands. There are young girls and grown women alike wearing homemade T-shirts with slogans like "I Love Hot Guys With Superpowers (and Fangs)" and "I Love Vegan Vampires." There are gleeful members from the online community Twilight Moms, whom Meyer had breakfast with that morning despite being at a signing until 1 a.m. the previous night, and grandmothers who say if they knew how to use a computer they'd start their own fansite too. There are women who quit their day jobs and now make a living online selling *Twilight*-inspired T-shirts and jewelry, and a teenage girl clutching a letter for Meyer that says the books persuaded her not to take her own life.

When Meyer arrives at the podium, her pale face and neck flushed from stage fright, she talks about her new novel and gives reach-for-the-stars counsel to all the aspiring writers in the crowd. When she mentions *Breaking Dawn*, the screeching starts up again. The grand finale that will answer once and for all the future of Bella's humanity has been the No. 1 best-seller on Amazon.com for well over a month. "I kept saying that there will never be another book in my career like *Harry Potter 7*," says Borders' director of children's merchandising, Diane Mangan. "Who would have thought a year later we'd be talking like this again?" With anticipation online hitting DEFCON 2—should Bella end up with the sexy Edward or the faithful Jacob?—Meyer is feeling the pressure. She went so far as to write her publicist a parody entitled "Breaking Down," in which she cataloged all the various ways she could enrage fans. "You have to understand," Meyer says wearily, as if speaking to her younger, innocent self, "that no matter what you do, people are going to be mad at you."

A few weeks later, Meyer opens the door to her friendly five-bedroom house in Arizona. Her husband, Pancho, whom she married when she was 21 years old, is with their three young sons at a water park. (He quit his job as an auditor at an accounting firm to be a stay-at-home dad around the time *Eclipse* was published.) When the tour for *The Host* wrapped, Meyer came home exhausted to confront the biggest deadline of her short career. She had just three days, working out of her home office from 6 a.m. until midnight, to make the

"YOU HAVE TO UNDERSTAND," MEYER SAYS, "THAT NO MATTER WHAT YOU DO, PEOPLE ARE GOING TO BE MAD AT YOU."

TWILIGHT
(2005)

NEW MOON
(2006)

final tweaks to *Breaking Dawn*. Releasing two books in one summer was madness, and she says she'll never make that mistake again. And yet, says Meyer, there was great satisfaction in proving to both her publisher and herself that she wasn't "just a vampire girl." In Salt Lake City her dear friend Shannon Hale, the Newbery-award-winning young-adult author of *Princess Academy*, congratulated Meyer on *The Host*. "I'm so proud of you! Because we're not sure if J.K. Rowling is a one-hit wonder," Hale gushed teasingly before the signing began. "But you're not!"

MEYER WRITES FACING THE KITCHEN, WITH headphones on to tune out the joyful antics of her sons, who range in age from 6 to 11. She used to have family photos on her website, but she and Pancho decided to remove the boys from the public eye. Occasionally she'll receive a fan letter at her home, which is unlisted, and those always go straight to the trash. And she's started getting random calls on her cell phone from fans, who stutter and giggle when their unsuspecting hero picks up. "Numbers are easy to change," says Meyer with a shrug. "Moving is harder. They'll have to drag me out of this place on a plank. Before I move, I'm going to put up a fence and get shepherds. And then I'll have a button and get to say 'Release the hounds!'" It's no wonder that Meyer is unwilling to let a few overzealous fans drive her from her Western refuge. Her parents live in the neighborhood, as does one of

her brothers. Best of all, her house has a spiral staircase up to the roof, where Meyer can find relief from the blogosphere under a blanket of shimmering stars.

At the moment, the message boards are bursting with dismay, fans having gotten their first peek at *Breaking Dawn*'s cover. Of course they don't yet know that Meyer herself helped design the image—featuring a chessboard with a white queen piece and a hovering red pawn—or how it relates to the story. "They just hate it," sighs Meyer, over cheeseburgers and shakes at a nearby In-N-Out. "After a while they'll like it, I think," she says, comparing the furor to the howls of outrage when Robert Pattinson was cast as Edward in the *Twilight* movie. "They freaked out and they all said nasty things and now all the taglines on their posts say 'When God made Robert Pattinson, He was just showing off.'" Harder to shake, though, has been the negative response to online postings of *Dawn*'s first chapter. "There were a lot of people," says Meyer, laughing and throwing her hands up in the air, "who said, 'This isn't the real first chapter, the writing is so bad!'"

Despite wincing over the occasional Amazon.com one-star review ("bookaholic," for instance, declares that *Twilight* "sucks like a vampire on your neck"), Meyer can't help but pore over the message boards. She loves her fans and wants to know how they're responding to her work. "Sometimes the feedback is helpful," she says. "I *want* to be a better writer...I read these other authors and I think,

ECLIPSE
(2007)

BREAKING DAWN
(2008)

Meyer at the *Twilight* premiere on Nov. 17, 2008, in Westwood, Calif.

Meyer with the cast at the Grauman's Chinese Theatre in 2011

'Now, that's a good writer. I'm never going to reach that level.' But I'm going to be a good storyteller," she says, sitting up a little straighter in her seat. "And what a thing to be!"

Meyer hopes the four-city swing for *Breaking Dawn* will be her swan-song tour. ("Though I imagine I'll get talked into it again because I'm a marshmallow.") Her big sister Emily, who lives in Salt Lake, remembers somewhat wistfully when Meyer used to greet 20 fans instead of 2,000. "It would be me and my five little friends, because of course I loaned out my books and got my whole neighborhood reading, and we'd go to the ice cream store, and she'd read to us," Emily says. "Those were the gatherings that Stephenie really loved."

It's a far cry from Meyer's recent stop in Salt Lake. She was in her fourth hour of signing books when an 11-year-old girl wearing a rhinestone-studded *Twilight* T-shirt leaned over the table to get a good look at Meyer. "You're, like, my favorite author ever!" she said, clapping her hands. "I'm a person who judges authors a lot, and I don't have anything bad to say about you. I mean, I'm really tough, I didn't even like *Harry Potter*." Meyer looked confused for a moment as to what the proper response to such a compliment might be, and the young girl peered eagerly into the author's eyes. "Are we going to feel complete at the end of *Breaking Dawn*?" she whispered pleadingly. Meyer handed the girl back a signed book and smiled. "I can't really answer that question for you," she said, her voice both cheerful and firm. "But I felt closure." ◆

Pattinson and Stewart
photographed by
Jeff Riedel for **EW** on
June 6, 2008, in Los Angeles

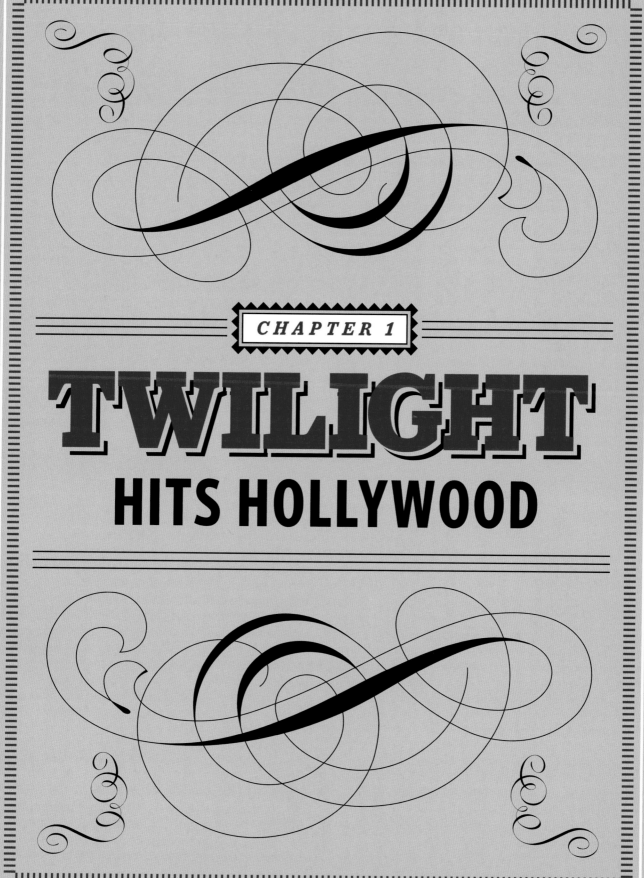

CHAPTER 1

TWILIGHT
HITS HOLLYWOOD

THE
VAMPIRE

*In 2008, **Robert Pattinson** gave us the first substantial interview of his career. He made fun of himself a lot, drove a junky car, and told us he ate only Hot Pockets. We liked him instantly.*

BY **KAREN VALBY**

LESS THAN A YEAR AGO, ROBERT Pattinson, a British actor known only for a small part in *Harry Potter and the Goblet of Fire*, was picked to play Edward, the brooding, beautiful vampire at the center of Stephenie Meyer's best-selling *Twilight Saga*. Fans revolted immediately. They were furious over the surprise casting of a relative unknown who failed to live up to their idea of the immaculate demigod from their book's dog-eared pages. By the time Pattinson's mother told him she'd read online that her only son was wretched and ugly and had the face of a gargoyle, the author found herself awash in guilt. "I apologized to Rob," says Meyer, "for ruining his life."

But teenage girls have their mood swings. It wasn't long before the *Twilight* universe—17 million worldwide readers addicted to the tortured romance between Edward and a mortal schoolgirl named Bella—embraced the 22-year-old actor. In July 2008, when the cast participated in a hype-building panel at the Comic-Con festival, all Pattinson had to do was smile or shift in his seat to send the thousands of besotted girls into fits of red-faced screaming. After the panel, the shaken actor bruised some tender hearts when he likened the sound of the collective squeal to something one might hear when entering "the gates of hell." Fame, clearly, would take getting used to. "There is going to be a group of girls who will follow his actions from now on," says Meyer. "I asked the producer, 'Is Rob ready for this? Have you guys prepped him? Is he ready to be the It Guy?' I don't think he really is. I don't think he sees himself that way. And I think the transition is going to be a little rocky."

For this story—the first in-depth interview of Pattinson's young career—the actor's manager suggested that Hollywood's next It Guy be interviewed at the Chateau Marmont hotel, in L.A., over a civilized lunch on the chic outdoor patio. So on a recent fall afternoon, Pattinson, looking slightly befuddled, wearing secondhand black jeans, what he assumes was once a rather large woman's bowling shirt, and old Chinese slippers with his big toes sticking sadly out of gaping holes, folds his lanky six-foot frame into a tiny chair. He speaks softly, hunched over his water. Tugging at his unkempt hair, he tries to explain why Jack Nicholson is his favorite actor, before admitting that he feels absurd. "Why are we here?" he wonders, looking around at the uptight crowd. "I feel judged!"

After ditching the hotel—"Okay, let's think, everything is all schmancy and industry around here"—he suggests a low-rent heavy metal bar in West Hollywood where he's sung and played guitar at a couple of open-mic nights. Pattinson, who owns every album by his favorite musician, Van Morrison, hopes to record an album soon. He laughs at what a cliché he must sound like. "Every actor I meet here says they're a musician as well," he says. On the ride to the bar, he apologizes for the state of his car, a rattling 1989 black convertible BMW that he recently bought for $2,000. The roof is broken, the old dashboard that caught on fire while he was driving on the highway is chucked in the backseat with the rest of his junk, and he insists that the red flashing light on the new dash is nothing to be alarmed by. "If I crash," he pleads with an impish grin, after nearly rear-ending a sleek Mercedes, "don't mention it in the article, will you?"

AT THE RAINBOW BAR & GRILL, WHERE the waitresses look like world-weary biker chicks, with back tattoos and painted nails, Pattinson orders a Pacifico beer and describes his new life in Los Angeles. The studio has him set up in a temporary apartment (outside of which there are always a few eager *Twilight*ers camped) where the only things he keeps in his fridge are peach

Pattinson photographed for EW by James White on Sept. 16, 2008, in Los Angeles

"IF I CRASH," PATTINSON PLEADS, AFTER NEARLY REAR-ENDING A MERCEDES, "DON'T MENTION IT IN THE ARTICLE."

Snapple and a freezerful of pepperoni Hot Pockets. "And I wonder why I feel so terrible all the time!" he says with a laugh. Pattinson has made just a few friends in town, most of them through cheesy industry events. "So the only people who I hang out with seem to be club promoters and PR people," he says. "I keep getting photographed coming out of these lame clubs. It's so embarrassing. There was a week where every single night I was going out and getting photographed by the paparazzi or TMZ and I realized 'Oh, my God, I look like a complete alcoholic!'"

Pattinson was 17 years old, and attending a prestigious private school in London, when he booked the part of doomed bloke Cedric Diggory in *Harry Potter*. After the film wrapped in 2005, his English agent pushed him to pursue similarly earnest roles, but they no longer interested him. Instead, he landed a lead as a troubled young man in the London stage production of the German play *The Woman Before*. "At the time I really thought, 'Wow, I must be great, I'm like f---ing Brando!'" he says. "I had this specific idea where 'I'm going to be a weirdo, this is how I'm going to promote myself.' And then of course I ended up getting fired."

There followed a strange couple of years where Pattinson lived off his *Harry Potter* paycheck, drifting between obscure parts in small films and TV. In late 2007, during a two-week run of auditions in Hollywood, he tried out for the role of Edward, a teenage vampire who is rich and perfect and princely in the way 17-year-old boys rarely are—and who falls not for the sexy cheerleader but the shy new girl in town. "I'd read the book and liked the book, but it made me really uncomfortable trying to picture myself in this part," he says. "Here's this guy who seems to be the embodiment of every single perfect guy. Okay, I'm going to look like a complete idiot if I just try to do that—like give a half-Fonz, half–George Clooney impression. I went in thinking I would just break into hysterical laughter. But then I did it with Kristen and it was completely different. We had this chemistry that just worked."

Two months before filming began, Pattinson went alone to Oregon, where the cast and crew would eventually join him. He pored over both the script and *Midnight Sun*, Meyer's unfinished version of *Twilight* that is narrated from Edward's perspective, determined to mine the deepest meaning from every line. In the book Edward is described as being all sinew and six-pack, so he spent long hours at the gym, shedding pounds at an alarming rate. "Then three weeks before shooting the producers were like, 'What're you doing? You look like an alien!'" he laughs. "Oh, well, I thought it was a cool idea."

Pattinson's idea to play Edward as a manic-depressive also made people nervous. The producers took to trailing

Edward (Pattinson) waits, Edward dates: (from left) alone and at the prom with Bella (Stewart)

PATTINSON'S HOPES FOR HIS CAREER: "I DON'T WANT TO BE AN IDIOT, AND THAT'S ALWAYS A DISTINCT POSSIBILITY."

after him on the set with highlighted passages from the book of all the times Edward smiled. "It was like, 'Argh! I was going to smile at some point.' Or everyone would be like, 'Well, let's try to make this bit funnier!' But it wasn't funny. I tried to play it, as much as possible, like a 17-year-old boy who had this purgatory inflicted on him. I just thought, 'How would you play this part if it wasn't a teen-book adaptation?'"

the cast was given prepared answers, but Pattinson refused to stick to the script. "Even little kids don't want to hear you say the same pat stuff," he insists. "It's boring! I'm thinking about my career in long terms, rather than just trying to milk one thing for whatever it's worth. You either have to be off book from the beginning or be on book forever. And I've never really seen the point of being on book." He laughs and signals the waitress for another round of beers. "Watch, though. I'm going to be completely destroyed."

WHILE PATTINSON IS ON DECK FOR any *Twilight* sequels, he's also trying to take advantage of Hollywood's new interest in his career. "It's funny how quick everything changes," says Pattinson. "Literally, the trailer came out and people who've met me, like, six times are suddenly like, 'Hey! It's really nice to meet you.' After having a big period of unemployment, you think, 'Okay, I'm not going to mess this up again.' So no matter what the meeting is now, even if it's for some dumb movie, even if I don't want to do it, I'm going to go to the meeting and give the most complicated character breakdown I can think of."

It's hard for a boy on the brink of stardom to answer just what he wants out of sudden fame. Despite his appearances now in two wildly popular franchises, Pattinson says he's not interested in grabbing at big-money roles. As soon as he comes into cash, he has a tendency to blow it all anyway. "Not on cars, obviously," he laughs. "I have very, very low expenditures, but still I manage to spend it all. I guess Hot Pockets are more expensive than I thought." He orders another beer and grimaces at his ringing cell phone before putting it back unanswered in his pocket. (It was his agent, reminding Pattinson to read the script for a Sarajevo drama and not to be late to their meeting with a casting director. Which he was.) "My only real answer, to be completely honest, is I don't want to be completely f---ed after this," he says. "I don't want to be an idiot, and that's always a distinct possibility."

When Pattinson was on the set of *Harry Potter*, he wrote obsessively in a journal that he carried around with him everywhere. "It was my diary, but it became more and more and more about requests to the Fates: 'I will do this if you provide me with this.' It sounds absolutely ridiculous, but I had so much faith in this little book. I remember one time I wrote, 'Please don't give me all my luck now. Make it all stretch. I don't mind waiting. Make it stretch for 70 years.' And now with *Twilight*—it was pretty lucky getting it, and I've been pretty lucky so far with all the attention, and if it's successful, then that will be a lot of luck used up. Maybe I'm just waiting for the point where I realize the luck has ended." He smiles ruefully, and rakes a hand through his messy shock of bronze-highlighted hair that the studio has forbidden him to cut. It's Edward's trademark, and he's stuck with it now. *(Additional reporting by Nicole Sperling)* ◆

Director Catherine Hardwicke could see that her star was torturing himself. "So I had a little thing— 'Rob, let's just rehearse the scene all the way through without tearing it down and criticizing it,'" she says. "We'd get two lines out, and then he would say, 'No, no, no, it's not working!'" Stewart laughs when reminded of Pattinson's inner turmoil. "Rob made himself crazy the whole movie, and I just stopped and patted him on the back through his neuroses," she says affectionately, then pauses. "He would punch me in the face if he heard me right now."

Pattinson and Stewart's onscreen chemistry is crucial to the movie's success, so the guy can be forgiven if he acted smitten with his costar when the cameras weren't rolling. "In the beginning I thought to myself, 'Because she's so serious, I've got to be really serious,'" he says. "I didn't speak for about two months so I would seem really intense. I would only ever talk about the movie. And I kept recommending all these books. It didn't really work, though. Then I started falling apart and my character started breaking down. I felt like an idiot just following her around, saying, 'You really should read some Zola—and there's this amazing Truffaut movie.' And she started calling me on things: 'Have you actually watched this movie? Yeah? What's it about?' 'It's about a guy on a train.' 'Did you just look at the photo on the cover of the DVD?!'" On more than one occasion, Pattinson was overheard asking Stewart to marry him—proposals that the actress, who's had the same boyfriend since she was 16, got used to shrugging off.

If the shoot had him in knots, Pattinson is determined not to be psyched out by the rigors of promoting a possible franchise. "I got sent to media training and my agent got back messages like, 'He's resisting the media training,'" he says with an amused shrug. Before the Comic-Con panel,

THE SCHOOLGIRL

Before Twilight *opened, we hung out with*
Kristen Stewart *in New Orleans. She was honest, self-assured—*
and convinced fame would be no big deal.

BY CHRISTINE SPINES

Stewart photographed
for EW by James White
on Sept. 16, 2008,
in Los Angeles

Bella outside
school in *Twilight*

SHE BEGINS WITH A DISCLAIMER. "I usually don't look like such a skank," Kristen Stewart says, fanning out 10 dirt-caked fingernails. Fresh off her star turn as innocent, lovestruck Bella Swan in *Twilight*, the actress—best known as the hippie chick in Sean Penn's *Into the Wild*—is researching a very different movie role at the moment, that of a young stripper in the indie *Welcome to the Rileys*. She's been spending time at a run-down strip club in New Orleans' French Quarter called Dixie Divas, taking in the show and learning how to gyrate around a pole, though she doesn't shed many layers. "I danced on the bar there three nights this week, and my legs are covered in bruises," Stewart says proudly. "Hopefully, the *Twilight* fans won't totally freak out."

Stewart has every right to be concerned. Ever since Stephenie Meyer's best-selling series of supernatural romance novels spawned a nation of *Twilight*ers, millions of girls (and their moms) have followed the first book's journey to the screen. Casting the schoolgirl was every bit as perilous as casting the vampire. Fortunately, director Catherine Hardwicke was roundly cheered when she zeroed in on Stewart to play Bella, a shy, ordinary 17-year-old Every-mortal. The actress' agents, of course, were doing backflips when they heard the news. Stewart herself wasn't so sure how she felt about being at the center of a cultural tsunami. She's still not. "It's just surreal to be a crucial part of a machine like this," says Stewart, over a lunch of raw oysters and po'boys. "I'm sort of the vessel. The book is what it is because of these girls' obsession with [Edward] through me. If I wasn't right, I'd be persecuted, and put on a cross."

Not exactly the breathless enthusiasm you might expect from a young actress in the kind of splashy blockbuster that could launch her onto young Hollywood's A list. Stewart is Kate Winslet on the eve of *Titanic*'s release or, at the very least, Shia LaBeouf pre-*Transformers*. But then again, she isn't much seduced by hype. "I don't want to do something that's just a big moneymaker," says the actress, who has worked steadily for nearly a decade but hadn't appeared in a genuine hit since her breakthrough role, at age 11, as Jodie Foster's daughter in *Panic Room*. Instead, she built up indie credibility by working with an impressive array of top-tier directors like Mike Figgis (*Cold Creek*

Bella and Edward

Manor), Jon Favreau (*Zathura*), and Doug Liman (*Jumper*), among others.

Stewart says she was drawn to the *Twilight* role not because of the books' ginormous popularity—"I figured it was a little cult vampire movie with a built-in fan base"—but because she liked the idea of playing a teenage girl experiencing animal attraction for the first time. "What I love about the story is that it's about a very logical, pragmatic girl who you think would never get swept into something that has this bizarre power."

After being cast, Stewart performed a pivotal love scene on Hardwicke's bed with the four leading contenders for the role of Edward, including Robert Pattinson. "Catherine liked a couple of the guys, and I was like, 'Are you joking? I can't do the movie unless Rob does it,'" Stewart says. "He *got* it, and we could, like, see each other." As Hardwicke puts it, "She would have strangled me if I didn't pick him."

DURING THE SHOOT, THE PAIR ENDED UP taking the roles—and themselves—a little too seriously. They spent hours deconstructing what it meant to be a vampire, and what it meant to be in love with one. The result: big-time angst, both on screen and off. At one point, the studio began to worry their young stars had mistaken this for a Bergman movie instead of a romantic teen fairy tale. "We were like, 'We're going to play this real' and the studio was like, 'But it's fun. Lighten up!'" says Stewart, who launches into an imaginary rant at the studio suits: "You knew what you were

STEWART LOBBIED HARD FOR PATTINSON: "I WAS LIKE, 'I CAN'T DO THE MOVIE UNLESS ROB DOES IT.'"

getting when you hired actors who aren't Disney kids! We're actually going to consider the characters, and not just smile on our marks, and hope we're in focus."

Stewart, who was just 17 when she shot *Twilight*, was uncompromising about what she'd allow her character to do and say. "We had to rewrite and improvise a lot of the most intense scenes, because Kristen will not say something if she doesn't feel good about it," recalls Hardwicke. "Kristen is very tough and she does not tolerate bulls---." Stewart just believes she was doing her job. "I had some of the corniest lines I've ever had in this film," says the actress, who was keen to tone down some of the over-the-top declarations of "I will die for you!" love. "We were so awkward saying those lines. Catherine was like, 'Just feel it and say what comes to you.'"

All this might sound like arrogance in someone else, but after spending time with Stewart, she seems like a genuine rebel spirit looking to do good work. Even now, as *Twilight* threatens to elevate her to the top of the marquee, she's not that curious about how far fame will take her. She'd prefer to chart her own course. Because she's got a kind of offhand confidence, it's easy to forget that Stewart's barely old enough to vote. She has an eerie calm about her for someone about to undergo a high dose of sudden celebrity. "For no real reason," she says with a shrug, "I just feel like it won't be a problem." ◆

THE NATIVE SON

*Once upon a time, **Taylor Lautner** was a 16-year-old kid with just one lead movie role on his résumé. But fans were already putting his name on their undies.*

BY **KAREN VALBY**

TAYLOR LAUTNER, A BOY WITH improbably shiny black hair and fresh-scrubbed good looks, was just 15 years old when he went to an open casting call. He was auditioning for the role of earnest Jacob Black, a member of the Native American Quileute tribe and Bella Swan's always dependable best friend. "I hadn't even heard of the *Twilight* series before I was cast," says Lautner, 16. But the martial arts whiz from Michigan, whose only previous major movie role was in 2005's *The Adventures of Sharkboy and Lava Girl in 3-D*, soon found himself thrust into his generation's most fraught love triangle.

"My favorite part of the series is the competition that goes on between the Team Edward and Team Jacob fans," says Lautner. "And I'm definitely Team Jacob. Edward is more intense and a little more uptight because he has so much going on inside of him. Jacob just lets loose—he's an outgoing guy, very friendly. And he's able to have a more open relationship with Bella, like a friend or even like a family member." (Careful, Taylor: The girl usually doesn't pick the guy who feels like a brother.)

Off screen, Lautner quickly bonded with his costars, especially Kristen Stewart. "He's amazing," she says. "And when you get to know him he comes out with disarmingly candid, wise things. He's a well-rounded dude who knows how to live life."

And he's already amassing leagues of passionate fans. Twihards, it seems, just can't get enough of his sweet, boyish appeal. "Somebody forwarded me a link to this site where they were selling women's underwear with my name on it," he says. " 'Team Taylor' on women's underwear. I was like, what is this?" Welcome to *Twilight*, Taylor. *(Additional reporting by Nicole Sperling.)* ◆

Jacob (Lautner) and his father (Gil Birmingham) greet Bella and Charlie Swan (Billy Burke)

Lautner photographed for EW by Jeff Riedel on June 6, 2008, in Los Angeles

"I HADN'T EVEN HEARD OF THE *TWILIGHT* SERIES BEFORE I WAS CAST," SAYS LAUTNER.

ON THE SET

The cast and crew camped outside Portland to bring Stephenie Meyer's beloved undead to life.

BY **NICOLE SPERLING**

ON A MARCH DAY IN OREGON, THE sun's as bright as a California morning. That's great news for the locals, but it sucks if you're a vampire. For two weeks, *Twilight*, the $37 million film adaptation of Stephenie Meyer's best-selling novel, has been shooting outside Portland—a location chosen, in part, because the skies are often overcast. Vampires, in Meyer's universe, can go out during the day but have to stay out of direct sunlight. Hence, today's problem. Director Catherine Hardwicke (*Lords of Dogtown*) has had to scrap an exterior shoot, and, because tomorrow's weather looks annoyingly cheery too, she's been forced to rush into an intense romantic scene between her two young stars. "We were building a bedroom in 24 hours," Hardwicke says later. "We were just sweating it."

Fans have been sweating it too. Not since Harry Potter has a book-to-film journey inspired so much enthusiasm—or so much anxiety. The movie will follow the novel closely: Pretty but awkward 17-year-old Bella (Kristen Stewart) moves to a small town in the Pacific Northwest and falls in love with Edward (Robert Pattinson), a heartbreakingly beautiful vampire. Edward also falls for Bella, but his desire for her barely controls his instinct to devour her. It's this combination of passion and danger, of course, that surrounds the teen romance with a halo of epic, doomed love. The girls who have gone crazy for the book have been vivisecting the film's development online. Two girls from the Make-A-Wish Foundation even requested roles as extras. "You can't make this up," Hardwicke says. With a fan base like that, all of Hollywood should have been jousting for the film rights. In fact, the movie almost didn't happen.

In April 2004, Paramount's MTV Films optioned *Twilight*, but then developed a script that bore little resemblance to it. (It featured night-vision goggles and transformed Bella into a hip track star.) "They could have put that movie out, called it something else, and no one would have known it was *Twilight*," Meyer says. Fortunately for devout fans of the book, Paramount put the project into turnaround. Then, in 2006, Erik Feig, president of production at Summit Entertainment, tried to make a deal with Meyer. The author had been burned before and resisted. Feig drew up a contract, guaranteeing

Pattinson and Stewart on the *Twilight* set

Director Catherine Hardwicke

The Cullens hit the cafeteria

the writer that the film would be true to her vision, including a promise that "no vampire character will be depicted with canine or incisor teeth longer or more pronounced than may be found in human beings." That did the trick.

Twilight is no garlic-and-fangs monster tale. It's more *Buffy* than *Nosferatu*. Hardwicke, who made her directorial debut in 2003 with the raw indie hit *Thirteen*, seemed an ideal match for the material. "When I read the book, I could almost feel Bella breathing," Hardwicke says. She hammered out a script with screenwriter Melissa Rosenberg (*Step Up*) in six weeks, then faced the daunting task of casting. The wrong choice would throw *Twilight*ers into a tizzy. Hardwicke also wanted to cast an actual teenager to play Bella, which meant finding a teen who could convey Bella's emotional depth and carry an entire film.

A S A CHILD, KRISTEN STEWART HAD starred as Jodie Foster's daughter in *Panic Room*, but it wasn't until last year, with Sean Penn's *Into the Wild*, that she blossomed. "Her mixture of innocence and longing just knocked me out," Hardwicke says. Hoping she'd found her Bella, she took a red-eye flight to Pittsburgh—where Stewart, then 17, was shooting Greg Mottola's *Adventureland*—and did an impromptu screen test with the actress. "She'd been shooting all night, but she learned her lines on the spot," Hardwicke says. "She danced on the bed and chased pigeons in the park. I was captivated." For Stewart, scoring the role was the easy part. She then needed to figure out how to play it. "The only thing I could bring to Bella was to be myself," Stewart says. "She's an honest, up-front, seemingly logical girl. She's alone but not lonely."

As for the character of Edward, Meyer describes him as "devastatingly inhumanly beautiful." Not surprisingly, he has become a heartthrob to millions. "Everybody has such an

Bella narrowly escapes death, thanks to Edward

idealized vision of Edward," Hardwicke says. "They were rabid [about who I was going to cast]. Like, old ladies saying, 'You better get it right.'" She almost didn't. Hardwicke had seen a picture of Robert Pattinson, a 22-year-old Brit best known as Cedric Diggory in *Harry Potter and the Goblet of Fire*, but had been underwhelmed. So Pattinson flew to meet with Hardwicke at her home in Venice, Calif. His audition consisted of a love scene with Stewart on Hardwicke's bed. "It was electric," Hardwicke says. "The room shorted out, the sky opened up, and I was like, 'This is going to be good.'" ◆

3 VILLAINOUS VAMPS

JAMES CAM GIGANDET
The scruffy vampire is an übertracker who catches scent of Bella during the Cullens' baseball game and targets her for his next meal. James ends up getting ripped apart by Edward and his siblings. Before *Twilight*, Gigandet was best known for his stint on *The O.C.*, where he tormented another hapless girl, Marissa Cooper.

LAURENT EDI GATHEGI
Although part of James' coven, Laurent tries to keep the peace with the Cullens, even bringing the family inside info on their enemy.

VICTORIA RACHELLE LEFEVRE
A redheaded bloodsucker with excellent taste in outerwear if not men, Victoria helps her mate James stalk Bella and launches a revenge campaign against her after his death.

Bella and Edward

"THE ONLY THING I COULD BRING TO BELLA," SAYS STEWART, "WAS TO BE MYSELF."

THE
CULLENS

EMMETT

KELLAN LUTZ

The ex-model and former costar of HBO's *The Comeback* plays the strong, jocular member of the Cullen clan— or, as Lutz puts it, the "protector." He's physically imposing and favors cold stares as the most effective means of communication.

ROSALIE

NIKKI REED

Reed is no stranger to teen dramas: She costarred in Catherine Hardwicke's *Thirteen* and guested on *The O.C.* before landing the part of Rosalie, the mysterious vamp who's reluctant to warm up to Bella.

ESME

ELIZABETH REASER

Kindhearted and maternal, the loving matriarch welcomes Bella into the family with open arms. But don't underestimate this mama bear. She will fight to protect her family when threatened.

CARLISLE

PETER FACINELLI

It was Facinelli's idea to have the good doctor and Cullen patriarch Carlisle (who turned Edward, Esme, and Rosalie) wear scarves: "Scarves convey the perfect gentleman, and perhaps there's a subconscious thing that he doesn't want to have his neck exposed."

ALICE

ASHLEY GREENE

The Florida native struggled to find roles after moving to Hollywood as a teen, scraping by with bit parts on TV shows like *Crossing Jordan*. With *Twilight*, she finally breaks through as Edward's future-seeing sister and Bella's vampire BFF.

JASPER

JACKSON RATHBONE

Call him the boy who can't control himself. Jasper, Alice's soul mate, has been a vampire since the Civil War and still has trouble resisting human blood—especially Bella's. Like Reed, Rathbone appeared on *The O.C.* in 2006.

FAN

Pattinson signs
autographs on the
red carpet in Tokyo
on Feb. 27, 2009

TWILIGHT PREMIERES
DEMONIUM!

BY KAREN VALBY AND NICOLE SPERLING

"PEOPLE KNOW MY NAME, AMBUSH ME IN PUBLIC, TRY TO FIGURE OUT WHAT HOTEL I'M STAYING AT, ASK ME TO BITE THEM, AND WANT TO TOUCH MY HAIR," SAYS PATTINSON.

"YOU ARE A ROCK STAR!"

The moderator at a Sherman Oaks, Calif., movie theater is paying homage to Catherine Hardwicke. The director has just stunned *Twilight* fans by appearing for a surprise Q&A after a sold-out screening of her movie. The audience screams as if Robert Pattinson just strode on stage and dropped his drawers. "OMG, OMG," the girls stutter, trying desperately to remember their questions. One 50-year-old woman asks the director what she thinks it is about Pattinson's Edward that makes women of all ages swoon. A *Twilight* mom in the audience shouts, "He's gentlemanly and caring and unattainable and mysterious all at the same time!" Hardwicke laughs and shrugs her shoulders. She says that when she brought her 70-year-old mother to the set she asked her mom if she'd like to meet Pattinson and his costar, Kristen Stewart. To which her mom promptly replied: "Just Rob."

The first movie to be adapted from Stephenie Meyer's break-out hit has left many, if not all, of the author's fans in a state of religious ecstasy. Made for less than $40 million, *Twilight* far exceeded box office predictions, pulling in a dizzying $69.6 million over opening weekend. "Up until this week, everyone was thinking this would be a one-quadrant movie," says a top female studio executive. "The men in this industry are still chasing the young boys—even after *Sex and the City*."

As the weekend's receipts were tallied, Meyer nervously awaited news that the adaptation of her first book was a hit. "There's that petty part of me that wants the movie to do really great so no one can say 'See, all this buildup for something stupid! Ha, what a flop!'" she'd told EW a few weeks earlier. Turns out her wish was her fans' command.

After celebrating news that the film had taken in more than

A *Twilight* fan shows some teeth at the film's premiere on Nov. 17, 2008, in Los Angeles

$35 million on opening day, Summit emailed a letter to *Twilight* fans, signed by stars Pattinson and Stewart, expressing gratitude and delight at moving forward with a sequel. But the studio still hasn't confirmed whether the rest of the cast will be brought aboard for *New Moon*. Fans are particularly invested in whether Taylor Lautner, who is markedly shorter and more boyish-looking than Meyer's description of his character, Jacob, will return to vie for Bella's heart. "We are definitely talking and thinking about it right now," says Erik Feig, Summit's president of production. "Taylor's fantastic as Jacob in *Twilight*. I think when we get closer to shooting, the director is going to look at everyone as if they are brand-new to the role."

And just who that director will be remains to be seen. As of press time, Hardwicke—who holds the record for best opening-weekend box office for a female director—hadn't signed on. But she spent much of opening weekend sequestered in meetings with lawyers, agents, and studio executives. She felt hamstrung by her modest budget through much of the *Twilight* shoot. "I had more elaborate stunt sequences designed and very crazy, cool stuff that I wanted to do," she says. "We had locations taken away. We had five days cut before we started to shoot. But, you know, I kind of got past that, I just had to let it go."

After the grueling production, Hardwicke now wants to make sure the studio shows her the money to properly tackle *New Moon*'s tricky plot-line—which includes location shooting in Rome and several characters who must realistically morph from teenage boys into werewolves. Summit's Feig has nothing but praise for Hardwicke, but he maintains that the sequel doesn't necessarily demand a bigger budget. "I don't think there was anything excessively lavish about

Stewart arrives at the *Twilight* premiere in L.A.

Twilight, and yet the world was fully realized," he says. "We'll do exactly the same thing with *New Moon*." Still, the studio might want to throw more money at the universally trashed special effect that was supposed to make Pattinson sparkle magically in the sunlight but left him looking merely sweaty. "People make realistic CGI dragons, so you wouldn't think making people sparkle would be that hard," says Meyer.

FOR NOW, ONLY PATTINSON AND STEWART are sure to live on in Meyer's fantasy world. But neither of the two young stars banked on this sudden explosion of fame when they signed on for the movie. Stewart in particular seems ill-suited for the rigors of sound-bite TV, as she fidgeted and frowned her way through awkward appearances on *Late Show With David Letterman* and the *Today* show. "I think she's had a lot of trouble," says Hardwicke. "She knows it's important, but it's not her favorite part of the job." Pattinson seems to have a better game face, drowsily mystified when teenage girls throw themselves onto his moving car or when Tyra Banks asks him to bite her neck on her talk show. He did have one flash of rebellion, however: "I cannot wait to cut my hair," he

told EW two months before the movie was released. "It's so annoying! I was at a photo shoot the other day, and people were saying, 'They say we can't touch your hair. You have trademarked hair!' No, I don't." And so, despite the studio's request that his ragged mop not be touched, he cut off his hair in between press junkets.

Fans will continue to debate whether Pattinson is dreamier with short or long hair, just as they wrestle over whether they love or hate the film they'd imagined in their heads for so long. "I went in expecting it to be crap and completely ruin my idea of the books," says Danylle Utley, a 31-year-old accountant and married mother who is the president of Salt Lake Twilighters Anonymous. "And it completely amazed me." She saw the movie three times opening weekend, including a Thursday midnight screening where she and 24 fellow club members dressed up in prom gowns and ate mushroom ravioli for dinner as homages to Bella and Edward's romance. "People think that I'm insane because I'm so invested with this fandom," she says with a giggle. "But they're all just jealous that the things they love aren't this big." (*Additional reporting by Dafna Pleban, Lindsay Soll, Kate Ward, and John Young*) ◆

"I've been to a lot of premieres, and none have ever been as big as this," Stewart told us at the *Twilight* premiere. "Maybe if I had been alive during the days of the Beatles it would be different, but I have never been moved enough to camp out for something." (Clockwise from top left) Elizabeth Reaser, Jackson Rathbone, Christian Serratos, Lautner, Rachelle Lefevre, Kellan Lutz, Ashley Greene, Nikki Reed, Stewart, Billy Burke, and Pattinson; fans show their love; Lautner.

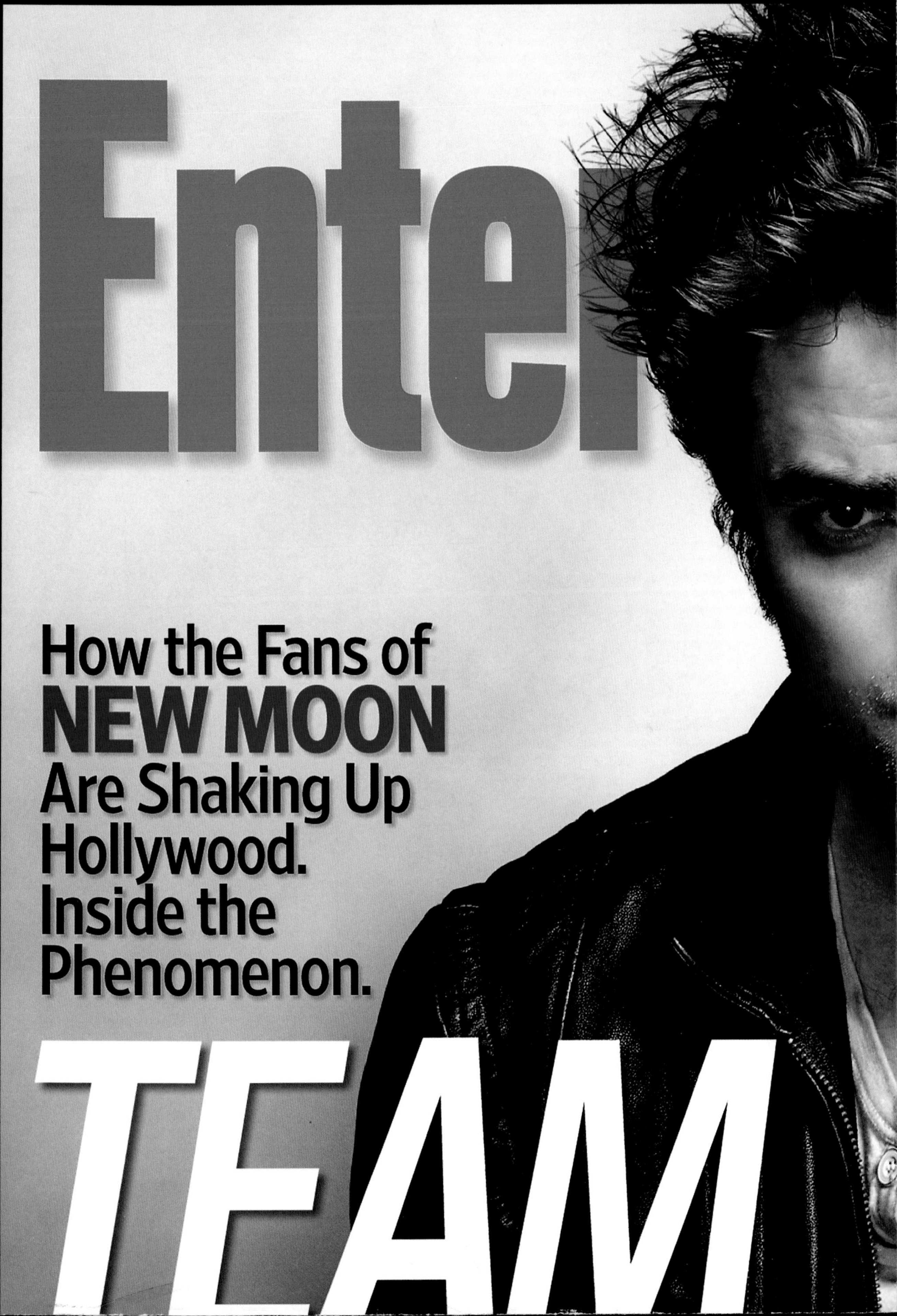

Enter

How the Fans of
NEW MOON
Are Shaking Up
Hollywood.
Inside the
Phenomenon.

TEAM

TWILIGHT
Collector's Covers
No. 1 of 3

nent
WEEKLY

#1078 • DECEMBER 4, 2009

BY THE NUMBERS

TWILIGHT

$192.8 MILLION
Total domestic gross

5,950 LBS
Weight of the 1993 Chevy Astro van that Edward stops with one hand in a parking lot to save Bella

50 mins, 56 secs
Amount of time elapsed in the movie before Bella figures out that Edward is a vampire

0
Number of gloves worn by vampires when they play baseball

7
Number of times Bella tells Edward that she doesn't care that he is a bloodsucking vampire who initially wanted to kill her

1
Number of cans of pepper spray given to Bella to fight off vampires

17
Bella's age

103
Edward's age

3 MILLION
Number of DVDs sold on the first day of release

$37 MILLION
Film's budget

$392.6 MILLION
Total worldwide gross

3,532
Population of Forks, Wash.

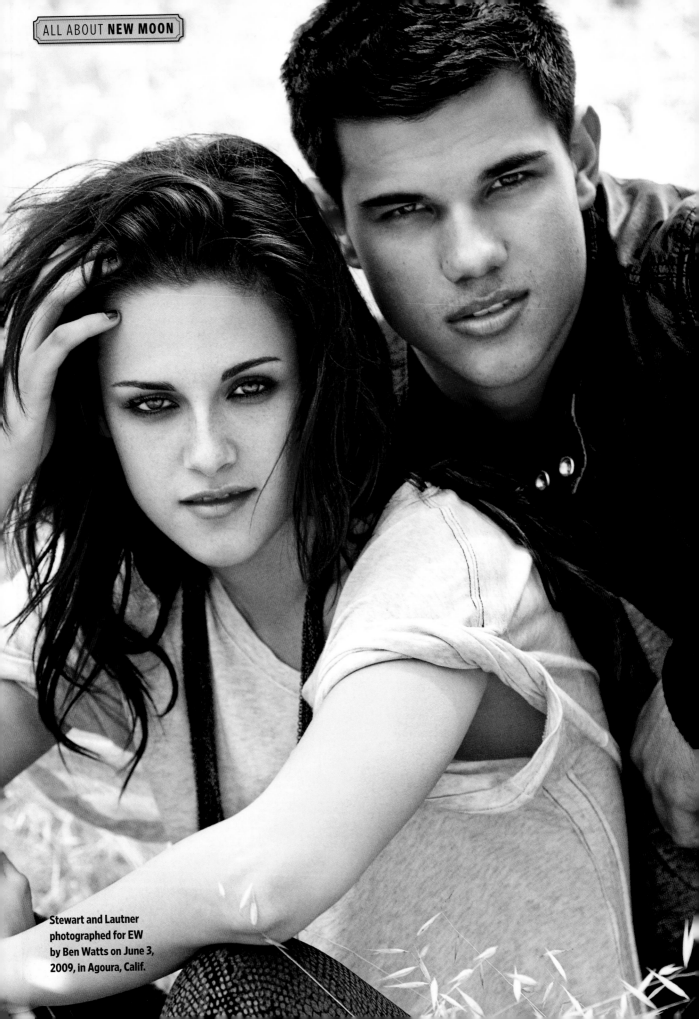

Stewart and Lautner
photographed for EW
by Ben Watts on June 3,
2009, in Agoura, Calif.

CHAPTER 2

NEW MOON RISES

HUNGRY LIKE THE
WOLF

Mere weeks before New Moon *started filming,* **Taylor Lautner** *still didn't know if he would be returning as Jacob. Here's the story of an actor in limbo.*

BY **NICOLE SPERLING**

BY THE TIME YOU READ THESE WORDS, Taylor Lautner's fate may already have been decided. He'll either be reprising his role as Jacob Black in the almost-ready-to-shoot *Twilight* sequel *New Moon*, or he'll be an exceedingly rare species in Hollywood: an actor accused of looking too young.

This week, Summit Entertainment is expected to announce a big casting choice for the next film based on Stephenie Meyer's wildly successful series of vampire romance novels. Kristen Stewart, 18, is set to return as Bella Swan, the beautiful human who falls for a soft-hearted bloodsucker. And Robert Pattinson, 22, has a lock on his job too; his turn as Edward Cullen, the hunky, soulful vampire, has made him an overnight superstar with young female moviegoers around the planet. But Lautner, 16, has a more uncertain future. That's because the character he was so perfectly cast to play in the first *Twilight* film—a slim, baby-faced teenager—will be greatly expanded in the sequel. And by greatly expanded, we mean into a hulking, snarling, seven-foot Lycan. "Jacob is a totally different character in *New Moon*," says Melissa Rosenberg, screenwriter of both *Twilight* films. "He's a foot taller and huge—and he's supposed to look 25. It's really a question of whether or not the same actor can play the role." Rosenberg is quick to add, however, that "everyone would love to keep him. We all think he's the loveliest person ever."

Lautner's certainly been doing everything in his mortal power to hang on to the part. Since *Twilight*, he's gained 19 pounds and is promising to pack on 10 more before shooting starts on *New Moon* this March. And judging from a widely reprinted red-carpet interview, he's not shy about letting Summit and *New Moon*'s director, Chris Weitz, know that he has the chops for the gig. "My job for *Twilight* was to bring *Twilight* Jacob to life—the friendly, happy-go-lucky little Jacob," he told MTV News. "My job for *New Moon* is completely different. I've been looking forward to that. I've been getting ready for it, and I can assure them I will follow through with that."

Fans of the *Twilight* novels—specifically those who identify themselves as "Team Jacob"—are divided over whether Lautner has the machismo to carry *New Moon*. In fact, pro-Lautner/anti-Lautner fights have been breaking out on the Web for weeks. As Rosenberg puts it, "He has to play a romantic lead against Rob, who's a 22-year-old man. That's a tall order."

Summit declined to comment on the specifics of this story, but *Twilight* has so far grossed $263 million worldwide, and usually when a studio hits franchise pay dirt it tries to keep all the parts in place. Yes, there are exceptions. Don Cheadle replaced Terrence Howard in *Iron Man 2*. Nick Stahl took over for Edward Furlong as John Connor in *Terminator 3*, while Jake Gyllenhaal very nearly stole *Spider-Man 2* out from under Tobey Maguire. Recently, there have been rumors that Michael Copon (*The Scorpion King 2*) and Steven Strait (*10,000 BC*) are jockeying for Lautner's spot. But you can chalk that up to empty Web noise: Reps for both actors say neither has been approached for the role. In fact, in what may shape up to be a triumph of the underdog, sources close to the production say that the simplest route would be to go with Lautner. EW has confirmed that the actor has not only met with director Weitz, but was even screen-tested for chemistry with Stewart. "I'm very hopeful," a *New Moon* insider says of Lautner. "We're not looking at anybody else."

The irony, it turns out, is that Summit went to an awful lot of trouble to find Lautner in the first place. In late 2007, the studio launched a nationwide campaign, auditioning hundreds of hopefuls in a search for just the right Native American actor to play Jacob Black. They never did find one—Lautner, turns out, is French, Dutch, and German—but it was a lot of work. Of course, nobody back then could have anticipated just how huge a phenomenon the first *Twilight* movie would become—or how much would end up riding on the casting of its sequel. Even if Lautner does keep his job, he may be nervous enough to start pulling his fur out. ◆

Lautner photographed for EW by Ben Watts on June 3, 2009, in Agoura, Calif.

"JACOB IS A TOTALLY DIFFERENT CHARACTER IN *NEW MOON*," SAYS ROSENBERG. "IT'S REALLY A QUESTION OF WHETHER THE SAME ACTOR CAN PLAY THE ROLE."

NEW MOVIE,
NEW LOVE?

With Lautner on board, the love triangle heated up.

BY **NICOLE SPERLING**

KRISTEN STEWART LIES ON A BEIGE carpet, surrounded by a mess of pink roses and broken crystal. Her sweater is ripped, revealing a bloody gash on her right arm. It's April in Vancouver, and the *New Moon* cast is filming Bella Swan's climactic 18th-birthday celebration—the one cut short after an innocent paper cut turns the Cullen family from civilized "vegetarian" vampires into six beastly creatures hungry for sweet human blood. Director Chris Weitz wants another take of Edward (Robert Pattinson) fighting off his vampire brother Jasper (Jackson Rathbone), as Stewart lies injured in the background. This is the third freezing night in a row that the cast has worked until dawn, but that doesn't stop the set from feeling warm and jovial. Pattinson mugs for the movie camera between takes and teases his costar for just lying on the floor in the midst of all the vamp-on-vamp violence. "Do you want Kristen to give us a little life back there?" he jokes to the director. Kristen smiles. "I'm just writhing down here," she says. "A lot of writhing. I writhe really well."

So do *Twilight* fans. Right now, millions around the world are writhing in delicious agony as they wait for *New Moon* to hit theaters. Last year *Twilight* grossed close to $400 million worldwide and set Stewart and Pattinson on the road to superstardom—and superscrutiny. Now the team is back with *New Moon*, though the sequel is a different beast—and one that's not as easy to tame. Meyer's second book is steeped in heartbreak and sadness, focusing on Bella's road to recovery after Edward smashes her heart into a million pieces and then vanishes. In addition to the melodrama, the movie has to make do with very little of the dreamy Edward Cullen. Instead, it mainly concerns the burgeoning relationship between Bella and her friend Jacob (Taylor Lautner), who transforms into a gnarling werewolf. Pattinson couldn't be happier with his downsized role. "It was a stress-free job for three months," says the actor in his charming British lilt. "All the pressure was on Taylor."

In truth, no one in *Twilight*-world should be feeling any pain. Sure, there have been some minicontroversies. First, director Weitz (*The Golden Compass*) replaced *Twilight* helmer Catherine Hardwicke. Then Lautner publicly campaigned to keep the role of Jacob as the character grew deeper (and taller). And recently, actress Rachelle Lefevre, who plays the vengeful redheaded vampire Victoria, was replaced by Bryce Dallas Howard for the third film in the series, *Eclipse*. Each of these flaps rattled fans—but seemingly only strengthened their commitment to the franchise. Perhaps that's why the set feels a bit like summer camp—albeit a very cold, very dark summer camp filled with vampires and blood. "In a weird way, there is less pressure this time around, since it's something we know people want to see," says producer Wyck Godfrey.

Stewart and Lautner photographed for EW by Ben Watts on June 3, 2009, in Agoura, Calif.

Weitz replaced Hardwicke mere weeks after *Twilight* became a box office sensation. Depending on whom you talk to, Hardwicke left the franchise either because of a scheduling conflict or because she wanted, among other things, a bigger budget for *New Moon* and more time to shoot it. What no one debates is that the studio needed a director who could handle the expanded scope of the sequel, which called for hulking werewolves and a location shoot in Italy. Summit also wanted a filmmaker well versed in special effects, particularly after the first movie was ridiculed for the

"I LOVE THAT KID," STEWART SAYS OF LAUTNER. "I'D KILL FOR HIM, LITERALLY."

scene in which Edward's skin is exposed to sunlight and begins sparkling like he's in a weird body-lotion commercial.

Weitz had the right F/X cred for the job. The Cambridge grad had spent three years overseeing the otherworldly creatures in his 2007 adaptation of Philip Pullman's *The Golden Compass*. The film didn't score with most critics, but its visual effects won an Oscar. So, with the exception of being, you know, male, Weitz seemed a good fit for *New Moon*. Aware that his gender is a sticking point with many fans, the director, talking on set between takes,

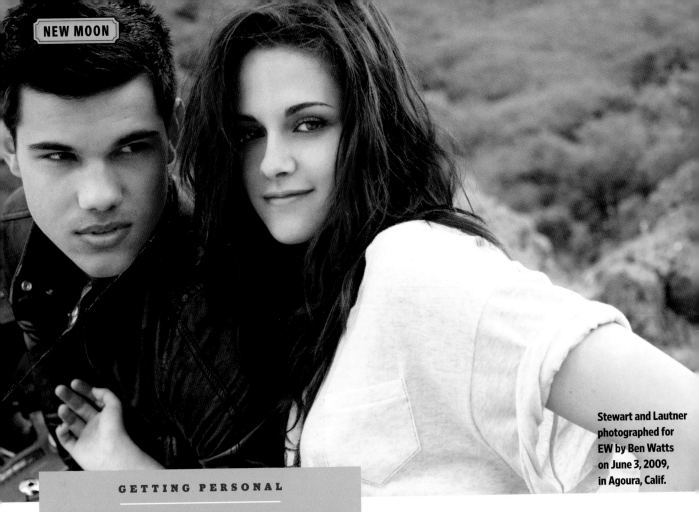

Stewart and Lautner photographed for EW by Ben Watts on June 3, 2009, in Agoura, Calif.

GETTING PERSONAL

KRISTEN STEWART

ON DOING INTERVIEWS "Self-evaluation is not my strong point, and you're constantly asked to critique yourself. You just spent three months on a set and your whole life is wrapped up in that—and then it's like, 'Okay, define that right now in five seconds.' I can't do that. I used to get so nervous that I would become a completely different person—and then they would think that that was me. [*Laughs*] So I've tried to calm down, but no one's ever going to write, 'Oh, she's actually just a pretty f---in' average chick who really loves what she does.' That's not gonna happen."

ON TABLOID SPECULATION "It's so absurd. I walk out of my trailer with my pants undone—and they think I'm pregnant? I mean, really?! [*She looks down at her stomach.*] They think I'm pregnant? Come on! [*Laughs*] Like, dude, I don't get it."

ON ELUDING THE PAPARAZZI "It's hard. I don't want to give my secrets away, but you, like, sit low in cars. And then you go into an underground parking garage and get into another car—and then you can leave. Once I'm away, I'm fine. I can totally go out. A couple random people might say, 'Oh my God, you're Bella in *Twilight*.' But I keep a pretty low profile."

downplays his testosterone levels. "I've always made movies for women," he says. "I'm in the more girly gradient of male directors. The thing I'm least interested in is blowing stuff up."

The moment Weitz was hired, he was thrown into the discussion about whether Lautner should reprise his role as Jacob. The filmmakers eventually tapped Lautner again, partly because he had a fan not just in Weitz but in Stewart. "It's completely understandable why they wanted to make sure he was right," says the actress. "But I knew he *had* [to do] it. Just because of how I felt around him. I literally saw Jacob in him." And how did the Bella-Jacob chemistry play out on set? "We have that relationship," she says. "It's lamely cute. I love that kid. I would do anything for him. I'd kill for him, literally."

NEEDLESS TO SAY, LAUTNER IS THRILLED TO be on board. He talks giddily about standing shirtless under freezing rain towers, and about the number of stunts he gets to do, but it's clear that the biggest challenge was turning werewolf. "Sometimes we'll film two scenes in one day, one pretransformation and one post-," says Lautner. "So I have to change my mind-set: Okay, I'm little Jacob-poo—and now I'm a big bad wolf."

From the looks of things on the set, Lautner will delight the contingent of fans known as Team Jacob. The Michigan native has packed 32 pounds onto his frame, downing protein shakes and other high-calorie foods during an intense 11-month training. But what may shock moviegoers—if they can stop gazing at his abs long enough—is that it

Edward and Bella confront Jacob's big bad wolf

"I THINK TAYLOR WILL SURPRISE PEOPLE," SAYS WEITZ. "HE DELIVERS."

seems the guy can actually act. "I think that Taylor is really going to surprise people in the movie," says Weitz over coffee, three weeks before he's due to finish editing the picture. "People have seen his body and it's a shocker because it's hard to believe that anyone can be quite so carved. But he actually delivers a really great performance. He wasn't just exercising all day, he was also reading the book quite a lot."

Stewart can be a pretty serious bookworm herself. At this point, she may know Bella as well as Meyer does, and, like many on the set, she won't let anything, not a director nor a script, trample on the author's original intentions. "We definitely feel protective of the series," says the actress, who has no problem stopping a scene if a note rings false. "The directors are interchangeable, so while it's exciting to have new opinions, at the same time it's like, 'Look, this has way more to do with what we have already created.'"

While making the first movie, Summit kept urging Stewart and Pattinson to ease up on the teenage angst. Now Stewart's diving headlong into heartache. She says she reached her breaking point one long, cold night in the forest while filming the pivotal scene where Edward abandons her. "Before the scene, I was sitting in my car, like f---ing crying— crying so hard you can't breathe," she says. "Because I was really overwhelmed and intimidated by the scene. Everyone says, 'She better be able to pull off the emotion in this movie!' And it's such an important moment in the book, when he leaves." The scene exhausted her. "I'm thinking, 'We have to be done now,'" she remembers. "'Just tell me we're done.'"

Despite the heavy emotional weather in *New Moon*, Weitz remained calm and contemplative, as different from the driven, frenetic Hardwicke as Jacob is from Edward. On particularly tough days, Weitz wore a shirt bearing the WWII British propaganda slogan "Keep Calm and Carry On." Sometimes he'd sit in the director's chair and read sci-fi

novels while the crew readied the next shot. "[Making *Twilight*] was much more of a fight," says Stewart. "Everyone was a little more scared. We needed to make something commercial but stay true to the book. We didn't have as much money. It was all very impulsive, and that's what I love about that f---ing movie."

She pauses. "But I think *New Moon* is gonna be even better." ◆

Pattinson and
Stewart take
direction from
Chris Weitz

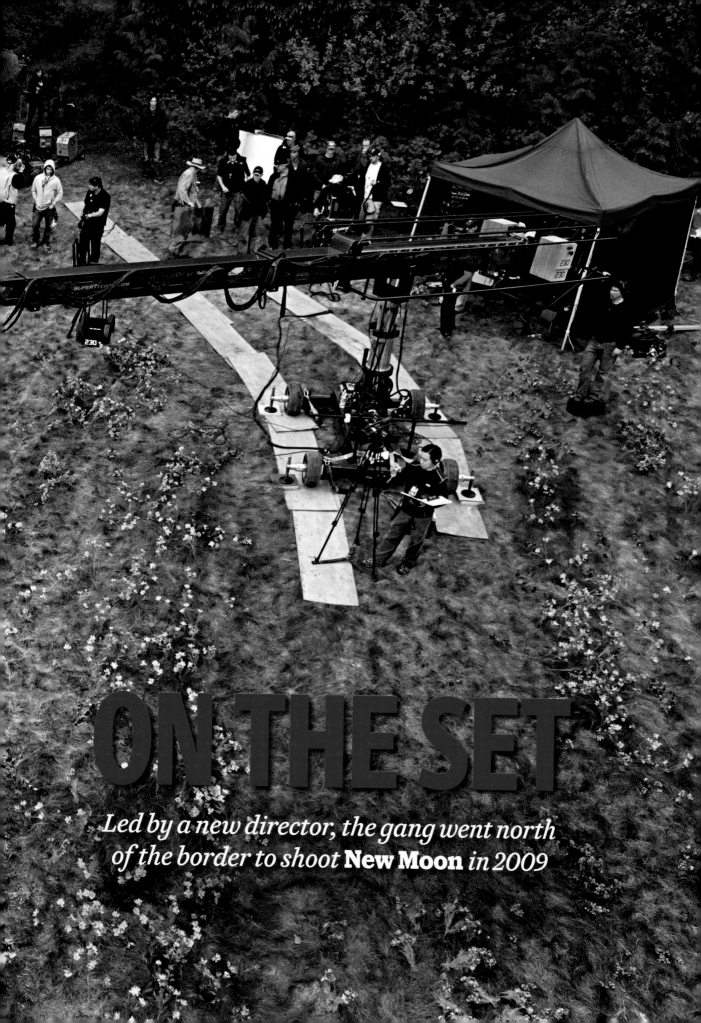

ON THE SET

Led by a new director, the gang went north of the border to shoot **New Moon** *in 2009*

S HOOTING *NEW MOON* WASN'T ALL DREAMY ENCOUNTERS
on the beach, like the scene you see in this picture. In spring 2009, the
cast and crew left behind sunny California and slightly less sunny
Oregon, where *Twilight* filmed, to set up a new base camp in the fog-
laden, not-very-sunny-at-all Vancouver. And during the 50-day shoot, the
New Moon team was routinely tested by moody weather and grueling
night shoots. "The lows had to be shooting at 5 a.m. in a forest and
struggling to get certain shots so a sequence would string together properly," says
director Chris Weitz, shown at right with Lautner and Stewart. "It was a very cold
forest in British Columbia, and we knew we'd have another night shoot just like it
the next day." Rest assured, everybody made it out alive. Says Weitz: "No actors
were harmed in the making of this movie." ◆

"She had room to run," says Weitz of Stewart. "She's a thoroughbred as far as actors go. Kristen's ability to manifest these emotions below the surface, above the surface—she's extraordinarily exacting of herself." (Clockwise from left) Weitz, Lautner, and Stewart get ready for a beach scene; Stewart has a doppelgänger moment with her stand-in, Mikayla Henderson; Weitz directs Stewart on the set in Italy; a makeup artist touches up Pattinson's vampire-red lips.

PAUL

ALEX MERAZ

Meraz says he had been doing films "in a breech-cloth on horseback, hooting and hollering," and saw *New Moon* as "one of the first times you see natives portrayed in a contemporary setting." The actor, born in Arizona to the Purepecha tribe, beefed up to play a werewolf. "I'm sure every film, it's going to be like, 'Okay, this is the scene where your shirt gets ripped off.'"

EMBRY

KIOWA GORDON

Though he'd never acted before, Gordon was cast as one of Jacob's lupine brothers after Stephenie Meyer approached him at the Mormon church in Phoenix where they are both members.

THE
WOLF PACK

SAM

CHASKE SPENCER

Spencer plays the stern alpha wolf in Jacob's pack. Born to the Lakota Sioux tribe, the actor (who appeared on the miniseries *Into the West*) lives in New York City, where he runs his own production company: "Through this sudden burst of fame, a lot of doors have opened."

JARED

BRONSON PELLETIER

The Canadian TV actor made his film debut as the frolicsome shape-shifter with incredible eyesight. Like Taylor Lautner, Pelletier followed a strict exercise regimen to get in tip-top werewolf shape.

DEMETRI
CHARLIE BEWLEY

The Brit, who plays a nasty Volturi, got a taste of *Twilight* fandom while shooting *New Moon* in Italy. "I almost had the shirt pulled off my back," he says. "And I hadn't done anything yet!" The biggest lesson he learned about playing a vampire? "The more angelic you look, the more unnerving you are wearing those red contacts."

JANE
DAKOTA FANNING

Fanning was the first big Hollywood name to join the *Twilight* family—and she relished playing evil as the sadistic, telepathic Volturi guard. "It's one of the first times that I've done that," says the actress, who'd always been a *Twilight* fan. "Jane is a character that really takes pleasure in causing people pain. That's fascinating to play."

THE VOLTURI

ARO
MICHAEL SHEEN

Sheen's daughter introduced him to *Twilight*—but didn't want him starring in it. "She thought her father was taking over something that was hers," says the actor, who plays the sinister Volturi leader. The actor stood out in the young cast: "They treated me kind of like an elderly uncle. I wanted to be down with the kids, but that didn't really work out too well."

MARCUS
CHRISTOPHER HEYERDAHL

The towering 6-foot-4 Canadian is best known for his season-long arc as the alien Todd the Wraith on Syfy's *Stargate: Atlantis*. He has also appeared on The CW's *Supernatural*. In the *Twilight* universe, he's the powerful centuries-old vampire who helped found the Volturi and who can sense characters' emotional bonds.

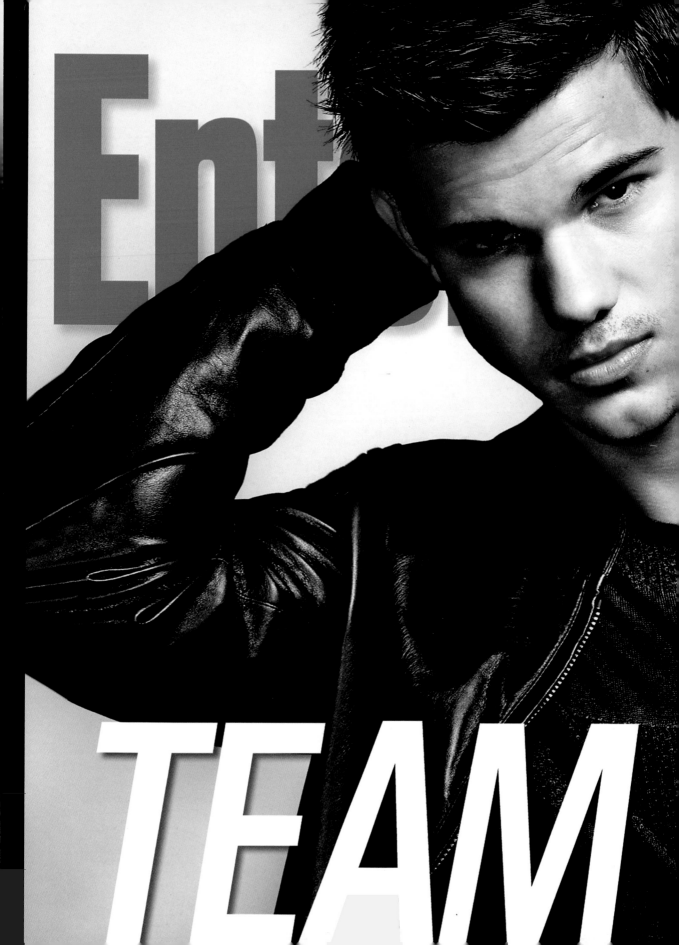

Ent

TEAM

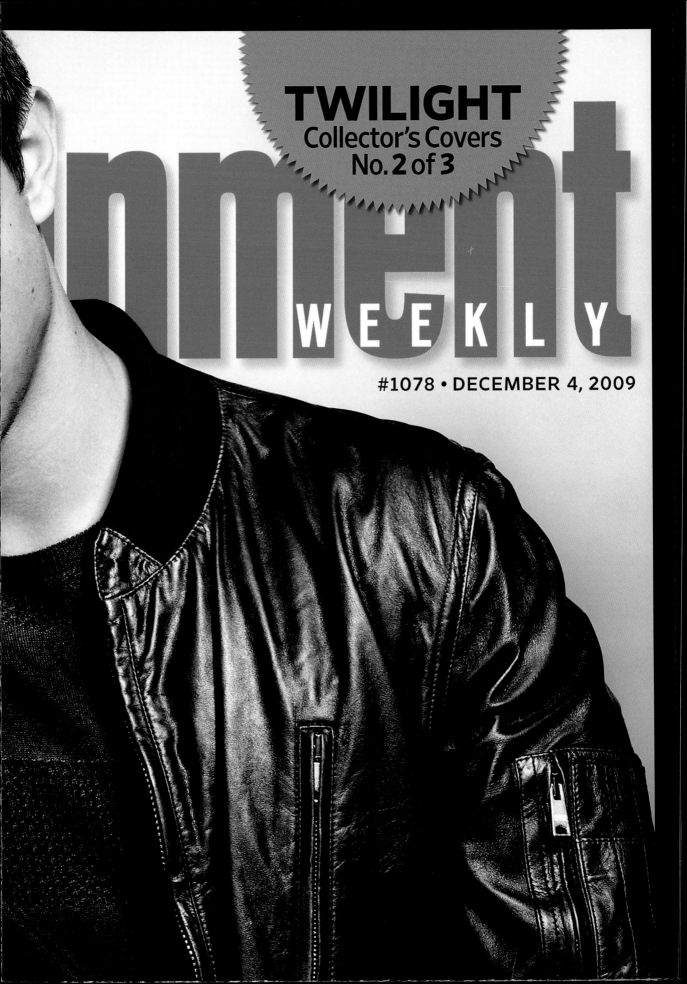

TWILIGHT
Collector's Covers
No. **2** of **3**

WEEKLY

#1078 • DECEMBER 4, 2009

ANGELA WEBER

CHRISTIAN SERRATOS

The So Cal native was a big fan of the *Twilight* books before landing he part of Bella's sweet, soft-spoken friend who offers support when Edward skips town and leaves Bella devastated.

ERIC YORKIE

JUSTIN CHON

Chon has described his character, the self-proclaimed "eyes and ears" of Forks High School, as both a "motormouth" and a "nerdy kid." Before *Twilight*, the actor costarred in Nickelodeon's short-lived *Just Jordan*.

MIKE NEWTON

MICHAEL WELCH

Known to fans of the late CBS series *Joan of Arcadia* as Luke Girardi, Welch plays Forks High School student Mike Newton. He is Bella's not-so-secret admirer and is jealous of her budding relationship with Edward.

JESSICA STANLEY

ANNA KENDRICK

Kendrick earned a Best Supporting Actress nod for her turn opposite George Clooney in 2009's *Up in the Air*. "George teased me," she says. "I was shooting *New Moon* at the same time, and when I came back to set, he'd treat me like a traitor."

CHARLIE SWAN

BILLY BURKE

As the shotgun-brandishing, pepper-spray-supplying Charlie, Burke takes the role of the overprotective father to the next level. he veteran actor—and musician, in his spare time—has appeared on everything from *Gilmore Girls* to *24*.

BILLY BLACK

GIL BIRMINGHAM

The Texas-born actor is no stranger to bloodsuckers: He appeared on a 1997 episode of *Buffy the Vampire Slayer*. As Jacob's wheelchair-bound father, he is the chief of the Quileute tribe and the man who brokered peace with the Cullens.

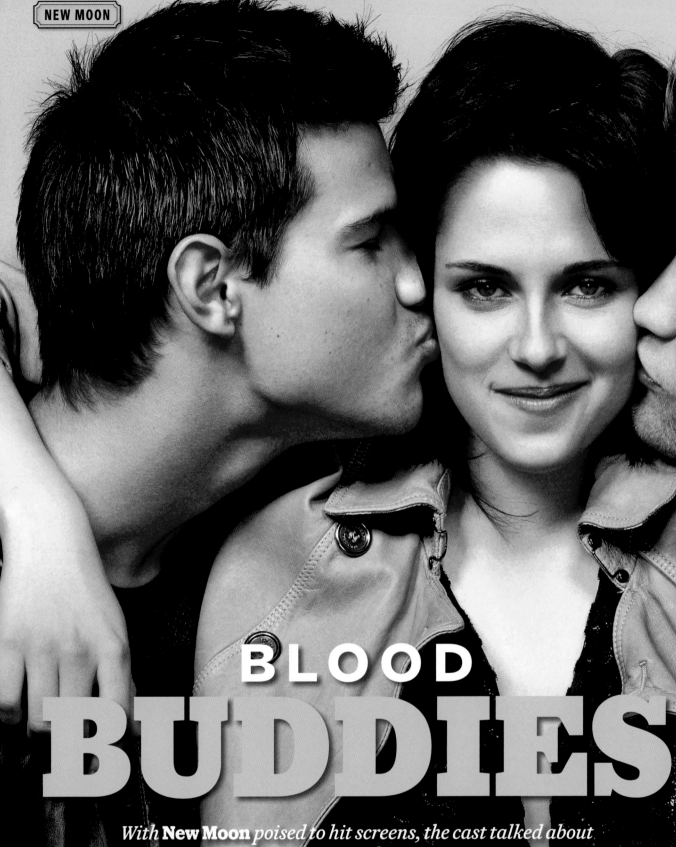

BLOOD
BUDDIES

*With **New Moon** poised to hit screens, the cast talked about
how their friendship had helped them through the craziest of times.*

BY   KAREN VALBY

The stars, photographed for EW by Ben Watts on Oct. 12, 2009, in Vancouver

F THIS REALLY WERE HIGH
school, they'd never be friends. The young stars of *New Moon* walk into the penthouse suite of a Vancouver hotel that has served as home base during the shooting of *Eclipse*, the third film to be adapted from Stephenie Meyer's vampire romance novels. On the streets below, newsstands are covered with magazines speculating about a supposedly torrid offscreen romance between Kristen Stewart and Robert Pattinson. One even declares that the two have moved in together and are nesting like an old married couple. Alas, their home is actually this hotel, which they share with thousands of roommates. "Yes," smirks Stewart. "You're sleeping over at our house now. Welcome."

Stewart, 19, who plays Meyer's moody heroine Bella, has thrown her dyed black hair into a haphazard ponytail. Pattinson, 23, who plays undead dreamboat Edward Cullen, looks bleary-eyed and rumpled underneath a New York Yankees cap. Taylor Lautner, 17, who secured his role as Bella's pining best friend Jacob by packing on 32 pounds of muscle, is well-scrubbed and wearing a fitted leather jacket. He is religious about his ChapStick. Yes, these three admit they would have eaten at different lunch tables in the school cafeteria. But in the *Twilight* universe, they are a united front, with an affection for one another that's undeniable.

How are you all coping with living in a fishbowl? Rob, you always come off as kind of amused by everything.
ROBERT PATTINSON It really depends on the mood. When I met you last year [before *Twilight* came out], I was doing interviews very sporadically and I never got recognized. Now it's like anywhere I go there's immediate recognition. So there's more of a responsibility...
KRISTEN STEWART [*To Pattinson*] You're not just any famous person. Edward Cullen is such an icon. When you see people on the street, it's not just that they feel like they know you. It's like they *need* you. You can complete a very personal aspect of their lives.

PATTINSON Yes, so I have to go around completing people. [*Laughing at himself*] It's a curse!

STEWART I don't mind working every day. It's just, suddenly I have this other role. And that's really disappointing. All I'd like to do is go outside with a book and figure out what to do with the day. And if I can't do that, then I'm just going to sit in my hotel room on my balcony and chain-smoke. [*Pauses*] I'm going to stop smoking. I'm not such a good smoker, anyway. It's not in my bones. I'm gonna drop it.

PATTINSON The three of us have been working for two years [straight]. It does feel like your day has a shape just as soon as you wake up. I just forget what it's like when you're free.

Rob, during our last interview, we wandered unbothered around Hollywood before ending up at some little dive bar.

PATTINSON That was a different world. I miss that so much. The idea of going to an interview now, unaccompanied, and saying, "Hey, let's go to a bar..." Jesus Christ, I'd have so many [studio] people on my ass.

Last year, you couldn't wait to see Mickey Rourke in *The Wrestler*. A few months later you were sitting directly behind him at the Oscars.

PATTINSON [*Laughs*] Literally, when they showed me the seating arrangement I just thought, Why?! Someone is trying to make everyone say, "Who the f--- does this guy think he is?"

STEWART And the camera kept going back to them, and Rob's just sitting there trying to look serious.

PATTINSON That was crazy. I drove to the Oscars in my little old car—I don't even know where it is anymore.

Dude, where's your car?

PATTINSON I lost it! And I borrowed a fancy car for five days and crashed it.

STEWART Because he was running from the paparazzi.

PATTINSON People never followed me when I had my little old BMW.

You were adamant back then about not getting a publicist. Have you since changed your mind?

PATTINSON No. My manager always tells me, "Robert, you really need

"IT'S A TRIP TO SIT BACK AND LOOK AT THE SEXUAL OBJECTIFICATION OF THESE GUYS," SAYS STEWART.

a publicist." And I say, "Oh, but you're doing such a great job with the publicity."

STEWART [*Laughing*] His manager has to work 10 times harder.

PATTINSON [*To Stewart and Taylor Lautner*] Your publicists are really nice, but to this day I still haven't seen what the point is in having one. Other than getting free stuff.

STEWART Yeah, but the free stuff all goes through your manager now.

PATTINSON I never get any free stuff! But I do catch [my manager] wearing a lot of new things lately. [*Laughter*]

You've all probably learned by now that ambivalence doesn't always play well in the press. Here's a chance to say what is purely amazing about enormous fame. [Long pause]

STEWART I mean... [*Laughter*]

TAYLOR LAUTNER To be honest, I really enjoy being up here. The filming process. Meeting new people.

Taylor, you almost lost a shot at being in the sequels. Do you have a different relationship with fame because you had to fight for your job?

LAUTNER No.

I was sure you'd say yes!

LAUTNER No, I kept my eye on the prize 100 percent of the time. I was motivated. I wasn't even thinking about anything else.

STEWART Thank God you got the job. I wouldn't have wanted to deal with you if you didn't. After all those months of working out!

LAUTNER I just wanted to focus on what I could control, and I worked really hard.

You mean in the gym? Because I see your abs everywhere these days.

LAUTNER Yeah, the gym was a major part, but I really studied the books and the character, too. And it all turned out good.

I'm impressed you didn't indulge in moments of "Damn! This role is slipping through my fingers!"

PATTINSON Yeah, Jesus.

LAUTNER I'd be lying if I said that never went through my head.

Jacob jumps into action

Jacob and Bella have a heart-to-heart

STEWART The only people who were concerned and reconsidering him for the role were the suits. [*New Moon* director] Chris Weitz, even Catherine Hardwicke before him, the cast—everyone on the movie was rooting for him.

Speaking of Chris, do you all have a say in which directors assume the helm?

PATTINSON No, but he met with each of us before he had the job. That guy's a saint.

STEWART He's such a nice human being, he makes you feel morally dysfunctional.

Does filming feel different now that everyone realizes how much money can be squeezed out of the franchise?

PATTINSON The strange thing about the first one is that Summit didn't know exactly what they were dealing with. It was like a normal film. There were the books, but we had much more free rein.

Wait a second—you complained that there was no freedom to experiment with your characters last time we spoke, too.

STEWART That's true.

PATTINSON [*Laughs*] I guess there was a lot of fighting on the first one. The most ridiculous one on *Eclipse* is my hair.

STEWART That's so funny. I was waiting to see what you were going to say, and then...the hair.

PATTINSON [*Laughs*] I swear to you I've never experienced anything like this. It's every single day. In *Twilight*,

"THE GYM WAS A MAJOR PART, BUT I STUDIED THE BOOKS, TOO," SAYS LAUTNER.

they wanted me to have extensions down to my hips.

STEWART He's a liar. He doesn't remember. He's remembering how they made him feel, but they were just, like, down to here [*pointing to her shoulders*].

PATTINSON So I told them, "Look, that's just not going to happen." I said, "It looks like this already—I'll come to set like this." I sound so stupid, but in a lot of ways the hair is 75 percent of my performance, so in the second one I said, "Listen, I need to tone down the hair. Let's make it a little more real, a little bit more...Method." [*Laughs*] And then in the third one, I'm doing fight scenes and there's a strand going down my forehead and they're like, "We need to do it again because no one will recognize you! No one will know who it is!" I'm like, really, is my face that generic?

STEWART They want proof that you're doing your own stunts, man!

PATTINSON I have to look like the poster at all times. Just in case they want to use any clip for the trailer. Any clip at all! There were about

five people in different departments who, because of my forelock, ended up in tears.

Kristen, it must be nice to watch the guys' appearances get obsessed over for a change.

STEWART You know what? That's really nice.

PATTINSON I've never felt so objectified in my life! [*Laughter*]

STEWART Seriously, it's a trip to sit back and look at the sexual objectification of these dudes. I've never been asked to do any of this stuff.

PATTINSON We have to do a scene on the last day where it starts out with her attempting to be objectified—only to end up denied.

Ah, *Eclipse*'s infamous make-out scene?

PATTINSON Yes. It's so funny.

STEWART He literally says, "Bella, please stop trying to take your clothes off." While he's shirtless!

PATTINSON [*Assumes a haughty baritone*] "Please, Bella, that's disgusting! Leave the nudity to me."

You guys are lucky. You clearly all dig each other.

LAUTNER The amount of time we have to spend with each other—if I didn't like these two, it would be exhausting.

STEWART And there's all these people that we as a group don't like. So if we didn't have each other to...

PATTINSON [*Mystified*] What are you talking about?

STEWART This group [*pointing at their trio*] doesn't like certain individuals outside of it. That gets so wearing on a movie if you don't have... [*frowning into her chest*]. You need to have people that *get* it, and that are in your position.

PATTINSON You need backup. When there's so much money involved, it really feels like you're one person against an enormous machine, so you need...

STEWART No! [*Gives Pattinson the hand*] You're not a part of this clique anymore. [*Laughing*] *Breaking Dawn*, dude, you're out of the clique. It's me and Taylor.

PATTINSON Wait, I don't understand how that happened. I was being supportive. [*Whimpering*] Fine, I'll find another clique. It does feel good, though, when you have a genuine bond. I don't think you guys would stab me in the back or whatever. Right?

You had two months off this summer, between sequels. What did you do?

LAUTNER I was in L.A. doing...things.

Intriguing.

PATTINSON Come on, what'd you do?!

LAUTNER [*Sighs*] Just...meetings. And I crammed in *Valentine's Day*. And I had to maintain going to the gym or I'd have lost it like that.

STEWART Eating burgers. He goes around with Baggies of meat.

That's a horrible visual.

LAUTNER If I have meetings all day, I'm running around downtown and I don't have time to...

PATTINSON Eat your meat.

LAUTNER Yeah, so I carry a Baggie and it has patties in it.

STEWART Patties, ugh.

LAUTNER The worst is not the patties. It's the sweet potatoes. They get raw and cold and gushy.

PATTINSON Why don't you just go to a restaurant? [*Laughter*]

LAUTNER I pack my bags of meat, what can I say? So I was busy with meetings...

STEWART And meat.

Rob, you made *Remember Me* in New York this summer, where you were knocked into a cab by hordes of fans?

PATTINSON That was completely made up. I was walking across the street, and there was one cab going about one mile an hour and it nudged my leg. The story ended up being how I got hit by a cab because of a mob of screaming fans, [but] it was 4 o'clock in the morning and there was *one* person there—a paparazzi.

STEWART People were asking me about it at work. I was like, "What?! Trust me, I think I would know."

PATTINSON And then there was another time—apparently they said on the news that I had a drug overdose. The security guy saw it on TV, and I wasn't in my room, and he was like, "Uh-oh!" It's just so weird. I wake up and my room is too messy to order room service, and so I end up eating a pack of M&M's for breakfast—and it takes me about five hours to find it. That's my first five hours of the day. [*Laughing*] And then you see the news and think, "Who cares if he had a drug overdose? It would probably make him more interesting!"

Kristen and Rob, why do you think people are so obsessed with the state of your offscreen relationship?

PATTINSON Good question. That's a little thing I have to think about every day.

STEWART Maybe it's just my personality, but I'm never going to answer it. I probably would've answered it if people hadn't made such a big deal about it. But I'm not going to give the *fiending* an answer. I know that people are really funny about "Well, you chose to be an actor, why don't you just f---ing give your whole life away? Can I have your firstborn child?"

You don't think just saying, for example, "Listen, we dated for a few months, it was weird, we're better off as friends" would end the speculation?

PATTINSON No way.

STEWART People are deeply judgmental and I'm not strong enough. I would love to be like, "I don't care what anybody thinks." But I'm a very private person. And I think about every hypothetical answer: "Okay, we are. We aren't. I'm a lesbian."

Careful, you're writing headlines.

STEWART I've thought about this a lot. There's no answer that's not going to tip you one way or the other. I'm just trying to keep something. If people started asking me if I was dating Taylor, I'd be like, "F--- off." I would answer the exact same way.

PATTINSON [*Looks at Lautner*] Me too. [*Laughter*]

Taylor, this is probably an inelegant time to wonder how your relationship is progressing with Taylor Swift?

LAUTNER [*Laughs*] What she said! ◆

"I'M A VERY PRIVATE PERSON," STEWART SAYS. "AND I THINK ABOUT EVERY HYPOTHETICAL ANSWER: 'OKAY, WE ARE. WE AREN'T. I'M A LESBIAN.'"

THEIR HOLLYWOOD
HEROES

PATTINSON ON
RYAN GOSLING

"He chooses things that are so right for him. He's handled his career perfectly. He seems like a nice guy, so people don't give him any hassle, which seems completely reasonable."

STEWART ON
CATHERINE KEENER

"She does what she wants, man. She's amazing. She doesn't have to deal with preconceived notions and expectations. People just take her work at face value. She's great."

LAUTNER ON
MATT DAMON

"The Bourne series! But I want to do different things, too. Ryan Reynolds or Gerard Butler—they'll do the coolest action movie and then they'll do a romantic comedy."

Lautner, Stewart, and Pattinson work off some steam. Stewart had dyed her hair to play Joan Jett in *The Runaways*.

NEW MOON PREMIERES

FULL MOON FEVER

BY **KAREN VALBY** AND **NICOLE SPERLING**

Lautner signs autographs at the *New Moon* premiere on Nov. 16, 2009, in Los Angeles; (above right) fans at the L.A. premiere

CHRIS WEITZ OPENS THE DOOR TO HIS beach house looking like a wilted rose. He's unshaven, pale, and wearing clothes he appears to have found wadded in a ball on his bedroom floor. It's exactly the way you'd expect to find the director the morning after his movie *The Twilight Saga: New Moon* opened around the world to numbers no one thought possible. But Weitz isn't recovering from a long night of revelry. He's just exhausted. In the last 10 days, he's been in more time zones than the sun, on the last stretch of promotional duties for his movie. "I'm at the point of physical collapse," says Weitz, 40. "Hopefully I will now lapse into obscurity. That's my plan."

We can think of more than 140 million reasons that's not going to happen—all of them dollars. On opening weekend, Summit Entertainment's *New Moon* made the kind of money usually reserved for comic-book heroes and boy wizards, breaking records for both midnight screenings and opening-day box office. Nonetheless, Weitz won't make any grand claims for himself. "The degree of credit I can take is limited," he says. "I'm just the glorified conductor."

Okay, he's got a point. Those hundreds of tween girls (and grown women, for that matter) who lined up days in advance

Pattinson and Stewart (below) meet the masses

of *New Moon*'s Los Angeles premiere weren't sleeping on concrete to see Weitz. They were desperate for Kristen Stewart, Robert Pattinson, and Taylor Lautner—who, after campaigning publicly for his role, has emerged as a formidable heartthrob. As the teenage *So You Think You Can Dance* winner Jeanine Mason tweeted, "Contemplating seeing *New Moon* again so my sister Alexis gets a glimpse of her boyfriend! She'd jump off a cliff if Taylor would save her." And despite the scrutiny they're under, the film's stars still seem to appreciate their supporters. "I would rather spend tonight hanging with the fans than answering any more questions," said Stewart at the premiere. Pattinson added, "I don't know how the Beatles felt, but I imagine it was close to this. Very few human beings will ever get to experience the love we feel at *Twilight* events."

That visceral, obsessive amour for everything in Stephenie Meyer's literary universe has turned a $50 million teenage melodrama into an event that knows no geographic boundaries. The global take for the weekend? $275 million. Many critics, unfortunately, haven't shown the same enthusiasm. "I've realized I won't necessarily get good reviews for this movie," laughs Weitz. "Having swallowed that, this was

"I DON'T KNOW HOW THE BEATLES FELT, BUT I IMAGINE IT WAS CLOSE TO THIS," SAYS PATTINSON.

made for the fans, and if you don't get it, then you don't get it." Hollywood certainly gets it. Pop culture has been bursting with bloodsuckers of late, and audiences are responding. Witness the success of The CW's *The Vampire Diaries*, HBO's *True Blood*, and a slew of vampire novels that hit the best-seller lists in the wake of *Twilight*.

Summit still hasn't decided if the fourth and final novel in the series, *Breaking Dawn*, should be one film or two. If they call, will Weitz answer? "I'd do it for Stephenie, Rob, Taylor, and Kristen. I feel a great deal of gratitude for those people," says Weitz. "But I don't think I could do another press tour like we did. I just think I would die." Of course, that never stopped Edward Cullen. ◆

BY THE NUMBERS

NEW MOON

16

Number of times Edward appears to Bella as a phantom vision

32

Approximate number of pounds Taylor Lautner gained while bulking up

$296.6 MILLION

Total domestic gross

TONIGHT'S MIDNIGHT OF NEW MOON IS SOLD OUT

$50 MILLION

Film's budget

11

Number of months Taylor Lautner spent training and downing protein shakes

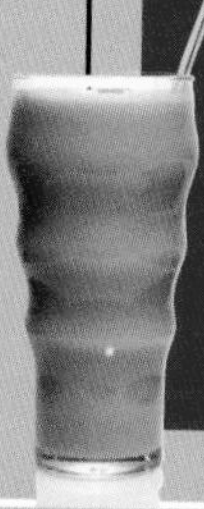

$709.8 MILLION

Total worldwide gross

2

Number of times Bella collapses from overwhelming sadness in the wilderness

6

Number of bloodcurdling, scream-filled nightmares Bella has in the movie

4 MILLION

Number of DVDs sold over the first weekend; 8.8 million have sold to date

7

Number of scenes with shirtless guys

108

Temperature, in degrees, of Jacob's werewolf body heat

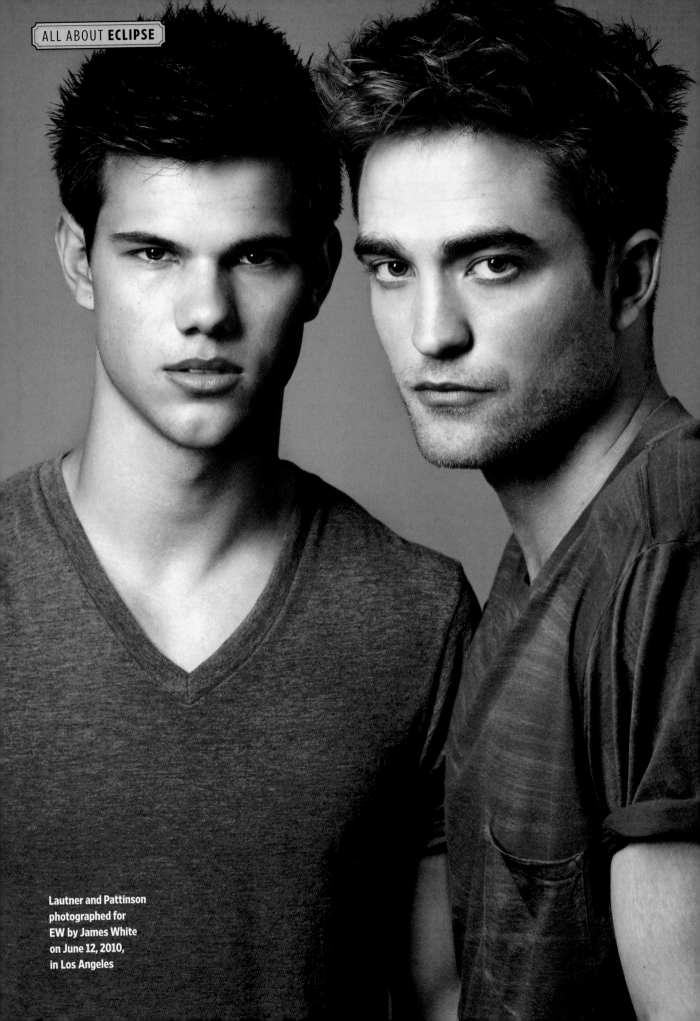

Lautner and Pattinson
photographed for
EW by James White
on June 12, 2010,
in Los Angeles

CHAPTER 3

TOTAL ECLIPSE

TAMING
FAME

*Stewart, Pattinson, and Lautner gathered in June 2010
to dish about Internet rumors,
freaking out at the Oscars, and, of course,* **Eclipse***.*

BY **NICOLE SPERLING**

KRISTEN STEWART comes bearing a gift. The actress—who's gangly, strikingly beautiful, and still only 20 despite having made movies for nearly a decade—has baked her interviewer a little loquat pie, which she carries in a mini–aluminum tin, like one you'd find in a child's Easy-Bake Oven set. Stewart and costars Taylor Lautner, 18, and Robert Pattinson, 24, have gathered to talk about *Eclipse*. At the moment, however, no one wants to talk about the movie—the darkest and most compelling of the franchise so far. They just want to try the pie, which is packed with fruit from Stewart's own backyard. "It's not warm and there's no ice cream, and those are really the two things that would make it exceptional," she says. "But it will be fine."

When *Twilight* hit theaters in 2008, Stewart never would have baked something for a reporter. Back then, she was a nervous 18-year-old who fretted over every syllable that escaped her lips and seemed terrified of the publicity circuit. Today, Stewart and her costars exude considerably more confidence. And they're a tight trio: honest, protective of one another, and warmly familial. In person, as on screen, Pattinson and Lautner's mutual affection for Stewart is the tie that binds.

How do you think *Eclipse* ranks against the other two films?

TAYLOR LAUTNER It is definitely my favorite.

ROBERT PATTINSON I don't like it as much. [*Laughs*] Could you imagine if I meant that?

KRISTEN STEWART It's always hard because you're so close to it. I run this really intense list of, like, checks and balances to make sure everything has come across. But I know I pulled less of my hair out [watching] it.

Speaking of your hair, you definitely don't play with yours as much in this movie.

STEWART [*Laughs*] No, because it's not my hair.

LAUTNER Nope, it was a wig.

STEWART I'm just going to be really honest right now: Yeah, I finally dropped my tic.

The emotional scenes in *Eclipse* play well, I think.

STEWART This is the first time that Bella actually indulges Jacob and sees that there are two very desirable paths ahead of her and not just one. It takes kissing him to see that.

LAUTNER [*To Pattinson*] Are you lifting weights?

STEWART Actually, he has been.

LAUTNER Seriously, he was just [*flexing*], and the bicep was bulging.

Is this to compensate for everyone talking about Taylor's body so much?

PATTINSON It is a desperate attempt. I've got body dysmorphia. I am stuck with my belly.

One scene fans have been dying to see takes place in the tent during the snowstorm. Jacob warms up Bella with his body because Edward is cold-blooded and can't do it himself.

LAUTNER The tent scene is probably my favorite, because it's the first time Edward and Jacob are actually able to connect and understand each other.

How many takes did you go through to get that scene?

LAUTNER Two days originally to film it, and then a full day of reshoots.

Why?

PATTINSON [The director] wanted it to be more erotic. Seriously.

STEWART It's true. In the book there's a serious sexual tension. As I'm sleeping, Jacob is staring over my vulnerable body, and he's naked in this f---ing sleeping bag because you heat up faster that way, and Jacob and Edward are leveling with each other.

Taylor, you and Rob have some major confrontations in this movie.

LAUTNER Some of those scenes were pretty hard for me. I think we ruined a

"I JUST FEEL MORE COMFORTABLE," SAYS STEWART. "BEFORE, I FELT LIKE MY CHEST WAS CRACKED OPEN AND PEOPLE COULD JUST REACH IN."

couple of takes in front of the house and in the tent. It's just, I don't know, I have a hard time looking at him...

STEWART Ha! "I have such a hard time looking at him"!

LAUTNER [*Laughs*] I wasn't finished. He and I were *thisclose* to each other—we are literally, like, an inch away—and we're screaming at each other.

STEWART And about to kiss...

LAUTNER A couple of moments it felt like that.

PATTINSON Every single time we had to do a threatening thing to each other—for one thing, you always have your shirt off, and so in the tent scene I literally grabbed your breast. And it's very difficult to remain in the moment. Also, in that tent scene, I can't really get over the fact that the word *thought* sounds like *fart*.

STEWART The word *thought* does not sound like *fart*.

PATTINSON It does.

STEWART Maybe because you are an English person.

PATTINSON The opening line of that scene is "Can you at least keep your farts to yourself?" I couldn't quite get over that.

Taylor, you worked so hard to get the body for *New Moon*. Can you ever let it go? Are we ever going to see a paparazzi shot of you eating a dozen doughnuts?

LAUTNER Yeah, hand me some of that pie. I will eat that right now.

PATTINSON I will eat the container.

LAUTNER I cheat all the time. I've got to be a lot more strict while we're actually filming, or when a photo shoot is coming up, but I'll eat some ice cream, some cake.

Rob, what's the secret to not having to take your shirt off?

PATTINSON Don't work out. I just kept telling everyone why I needed to take my shirt off in a scene, and everyone else had to think of reasons why I shouldn't. "No, I don't think so—Edward is much more chaste than that."

STEWART "He is modest. He is much more modest."

PATTINSON Then I'd say, "No, seriously—I would like to wear a really tight tank top and have my belly come out of the bottom. And have some sweat on it, too."

Would you guys want to star in a big franchise again?

STEWART I would have to love it like this.

PATTINSON It is just the promotion part, which is the hardest part. When you see your face on, like, toilet paper and stuff, that's when you know you have to negotiate the water very carefully afterward.

Have you guys become more savvy in terms of how your face and your persona are represented out there?

STEWART Well, you don't have a lot of control over your persona. Trust me, I've had a massive amount of experience with that one.

Interviews have always been fraught for you. What helps?

PATTINSON Knowing that it doesn't really matter.

STEWART And knowing that most people don't give a f---.

PATTINSON I would do TV interviews and I would be terrified, thinking that every single word would be judged. And it's really just, like, maybe two people on the Internet who are actually judging. The rest of the people are just watching, thinking, Oh, God, boring. You realize the [key to] marketing is just having your face everywhere, and that's it. It doesn't matter what you say.

Kristen, do you feel more at peace about being in the spotlight these days?

STEWART I just feel more comfortable, more myself, and I feel less bare. I feel much more like nobody can take anything from me. Before, I felt literally like my chest was cracked open and people could just reach in and examine and pick at anything they wanted, and it just freaked me right out.

You got a lot of criticism recently for comparing the intrusiveness of the paparazzi to rape. The comment got blown out of proportion very quickly, and you apologized.

STEWART I'm so sensitive about stuff like that. That is the one subject that means a lot to me. I made one movie directly concerning it and I made another one where my character has a horrible history of rape. I talked to a lot of people about it. I used the wrong word. I should have said "violated." But I'm young and emotional. It's just the way it goes

Choices, choices: Bella, once again caught between a wolf and a vampire

sometimes. I probably shouldn't say this, but I just feel like people got so excited once they saw that it was me. It was like, "Sweet! Let's get her!" And then for the people to exploit it under the guise of being morally upstanding is disgusting—and it embarrassed me because I was a part of it.

Did you see it all unfold and then think, I have to issue an apology?

STEWART No, I was in Korea when it all got bad. My publicist called me and said RAINN had issued this terrible statement.

PATTINSON Who's Rain?

STEWART You know, the Rape, Abuse and Incest National Network.

LAUTNER I thought you were talking about Rain, that Korean star, or something. I was like, What did they do? They sicced Rain on you? The Ninja Assassin?!

PATTINSON None of those associations came out and gave a statement [criticizing Kristen] without being called upon by the media first—who

and stuff, it made me want to do things. And you don't want to believe that someone you admire...

STEWART ...is an a--hole. Now they can't wait to call you an a--hole when you're not.

PATTINSON And any way that you can promote positivity—I know it sounds ridiculous—but it's the best thing you can possibly do.

Taylor, how do you feel about being in the public eye? You seem comfortable.

LAUTNER I get nervous, for sure.

STEWART He gets very nervous.

LAUTNER Us together—it's not good.

STEWART You make me feel a lot better.

LAUTNER I'm glad I do.

STEWART I am so shocked that you get nervous that it instantly takes mine away.

LAUTNER Yeah, it gets your mind off it. Like at the Oscars.

STEWART We were both so goddamn nervous.

LAUTNER I was standing backstage waiting to go out, and I could feel the veins in my neck just pulsing. I was like, Whoa, I need to loosen this jacket a little bit.

STEWART Literally, you are standing there in front of...

LAUTNER ...everybody you've looked up to your entire life...

STEWART Your whole life. And they're looking at you slightly baffled and saying, "What are you doing here?"

What about when you guys were on *Oprah* recently? There was a story all over the place that Oprah talked to you backstage and demanded to know if you, Kristen and Rob, were a couple. And that you said yes. Did that really happen?

STEWART [*To Lautner*] Did you see my interaction with Oprah backstage?

LAUTNER Yeah. I witnessed it.

STEWART She glided over to me—and she was strong, by the way, really firm hands—and she said, "How are you?" I said, "Good." She said, "Good. Are you nervous?" I said, "Yeah, I am, but I think I'm okay." She said, "Good. We'll have fun." And then she just walked away. And that was the most I talked to her backstage.

You didn't tell her you were a couple?

LAUTNER It never happened.

"I WOULD DO TV INTERVIEWS AND BE TERRIFIED, THINKING EVERY WORD WOULD BE JUDGED," SAYS PATTINSON.

were doing it specifically to get hits on their websites. That whole system of Internet journalists, where no one is called to account, is almost entirely about hate. All these people get away with doing it because they have no responsibility to anyone. All they need is to get a salacious headline and people click on it, because it's easy. And it's quite good being part of these *Twilight* films because you have to give so many interviews all the time, you can defend yourself. That's the only way. All of us stick together as well. There are so many little nerds behind their computers, on their little blogs.

STEWART See, if I said that? Cruci-fixion. You can say so much more than me. It's insane.

PATTINSON That's not true at all. When did I say anything [controversial]?

STEWART You're really good, but you could say "I just took a s--- on the Queen's face," and people would be like, "Oh, I love him! I love him!"

PATTINSON That is so not true.

Kristen, you obviously feel like you're under more of a microscope.

STEWART I'm a girl, and our fan base is primarily other girls. I would be the same way. I'd be like, "That b---- doesn't know what she's talking about."

PATTINSON One of the things that really annoys me about the rise of all these celebrity websites is that anyone who becomes famous—people are so desperate to prove that [celebrities] are lower than the average person on the street. Why destroy any hope for anyone else? When I grew up, looking at movies like *One Flew Over the Cuckoo's Nest*

STEWART Did [Oprah herself] actually say that? I don't think she did. Of course, when we go on *Oprah*, someone is going to say, "We got the scoop!" No, sorry, they didn't. I never told them anything. Why would I go tell Oprah that?

Rob and Kristen, you've both been making other movies. Being in *Twilight* must be a pretty good calling card.

PATTINSON One of the best things is how fast you can get a film started. I don't know how much longer it is going to last after the *Twilight* films finish, because now you can read a script and get it greenlit in three months. It's crazy. It's like having your own studio.

STEWART I still can't get *K-11* made because I'm playing a boy in it. If I were playing a pretty girl, it would be done already.

PATTINSON How much is the budget? I can get it made. Let me produce it.

STEWART Please do. There's this project that I've been talking about forever, and it just hasn't gotten off the ground. My mom and her writing partner wrote a script called *K-11* that takes place in a jail, and I would play a man. But people don't want to see Bella doing that, so they didn't want to raise money.

Rob, your movie *Remember Me* came out not long ago. Do you think it's unfair when people say, "*Remember Me* wasn't a blockbuster, therefore he can't do anything besides Edward Cullen?"

STEWART Like, "*The Runaways* was an enormous failure," which it so wasn't.

PATTINSON *Remember Me* was the perfect movie to do for such a short period of time. And I really liked it. I guess maybe it could have been marketed differently. But I think it did really well for a small-budget thing.

Is there freedom in doing a different role from Edward?

PATTINSON Yeah. And I think, Oh, I only have to do my job. I don't have to think about how the poster should be.

Did you find yourself thinking about the poster for *Twilight*?

(Clockwise from top left) Nikki Reed, Peter Facinelli, Elizabeth Reaser, Kellan Lutz, Ashley Greene, Dakota Fanning, Xavier Samuel, Bryce Dallas Howard, and Jackson Rathbone photographed for EW by James White on June 12, 2010, in Los Angeles

PATTINSON Yeah, all the time. No one ever listens to me. [*Laughs*] It's difficult now. On the first one we had so much more creative input, but now it's so huge that it's too big to steer.... And the other thing is, it's way too much responsibility. Why would you ever want that?

Taylor, you've taken advantage of the opportunities that *Twilight* has given you. What has this ride been like?

LAUTNER This was an amazing platform, and it gives you the opportunity to be picky and do what you want to do—and that is the actor's dream, to be able...

STEWART ...to choose stuff.

LAUTNER Yeah, and now I'm choosing projects that I'm extremely passionate about.

STEWART [*Fondly*] You cute-ass motherf---er.

What are you most excited about?

LAUTNER I'd have to say *Abduction*, because I start in three weeks. I play a high school senior who finds a picture of himself on a missing-persons website and realizes his whole life has been a lie.

What do you guys think of the career choices Taylor is making?

STEWART It's crazy how ambitious he is. I'm so different from him. We were on the plane and he said, "So what do you think I should do about this?" And it was concerning his massive movie, and I was like, "Dude, I don't make movies like that. I don't know."

LAUTNER It doesn't matter. She's an excellent person to go to for advice. I probably bug her because I go to her for advice so much.

STEWART Taylor, I would do anything for you.

PATTINSON Okay, that sounded like the most insincere thing.

STEWART See, you actually have a real moment and people just think that you're lying.

You guys are about to start shooting the two *Breaking Dawn* movies back-to-back. You signed on to this franchise before the novel *Breaking Dawn* was written.

"IT WILL BE SO WEIRD, THE LAST DAY OF FILMING THAT LAST MOVIE," SAYS LAUTNER.

When you read it, were you thinking, How is this going to be turned into a movie?

STEWART Yeah, definitely. What is Renesmee going to look like? Is it going to be this little teeth-baby running around? It's going to be weird.

PATTINSON [*Laughs*] "Little teeth-baby."

STEWART Yeah, but I think it's going to be cool. One of the main objectives of the series is to get Bella to a point where she's mature enough to make such a hefty decision, and she goes through a lot. In the fourth one she is going to become a wife. She is going to become a mom. She is going to become an adult and a vampire. To do it so young, it needs to be believable. So I'm really excited about playing that.

Some people read *Breaking Dawn* as very pro-life and Mormon because Bella decides to have her baby even though it's endangering her life. Did any of that bother you when you read the book?

STEWART No, because it made sense. Not wanting to give up the baby is about her holding on to that last thing that she would have to give up if she was not human anymore. Right after she and Edward sleep with each other for the first time, she says, "Oh, f---, I might want to be human for a little bit longer." The baby is just an even more intense version of that.

PATTINSON I think people make up all these Mormon references just so they can publish *Twilight* articles in respectable publications like *The New York Times*. Even Stephenie [Meyer] said it doesn't mean any of that. It is based on a dream.

The *Breaking Dawn* movies are the last in the series. How do you feel about all of this coming to a conclusion soon?

STEWART In terms of shooting them, they're almost done. We're going to be done by March.

LAUTNER It will be so weird, the last day of filming that last movie.

BRYCE DALLAS HOWARD
JOINS THE CAST

In July 2009, news broke that because of a scheduling conflict, Bryce Dallas Howard would be replacing Rachelle Lefevre as the villainous vampire Victoria in *Eclipse*—and *Twilight* fans went ballistic. Howard, best known for her roles in *Spider-Man 3* and *The Village*, is sensitive to Twihards' anxiety over the recasting. "It's sad for the audience that this disruption occurred," she says. "So I used the same costumes, props, and jewelry—everything I could find to make it a smooth transition."

STEWART It will be sad, too. It's been one of the most crazy, indulgent experiences as an actor, to be able to follow a character for this long.

LAUTNER I think stopping will be very weird.

STEWART It will just feel like a chapter has been closed.

LAUTNER A big chapter.

STEWART I'm going to be like, "But wait, there's this scene..."

PATTINSON [*Laughs*] "I know how to do the tent scene now! I'm 30!" ◆

ON THE SET

Just seven weeks after wrapping New Moon, *the gang got back together in Vancouver for* **Eclipse**

"It felt really weird kissing someone else as Bella," says Stewart, referring to her much-anticipated smooch with Lautner's Jacob. "I was like, 'What the hell are you doing?' It was a really strange experience—as it should have been." (Clockwise from right) Stewart and Lautner check in with director David Slade in one of the franchise's many car scenes; Dakota Fanning vamps as Jane, a powerful member of the Volturi guard; Stewart and Lautner go hand-to-hand on the Vancouver set.

ECLIPSE

ALL TOGETHER NOW

ECLIPSE PREMIERES

HAPPY CAMPERS

Fans set up tents three days early at the Nokia Theatre for the Los Angeles *Eclipse* premiere on June 24, 2010

(Clockwise from top left) Stewart smiles for photos with a grateful fan outside the Nokia Theatre at the L.A. *Eclipse* premiere on June 24, 2010; Kellan Lutz feels the love; Lautner cozies up to a Team Jacob member; Pattinson works the Team Edward crowd; new cast member Bryce Dallas Howard mingles with the masses.

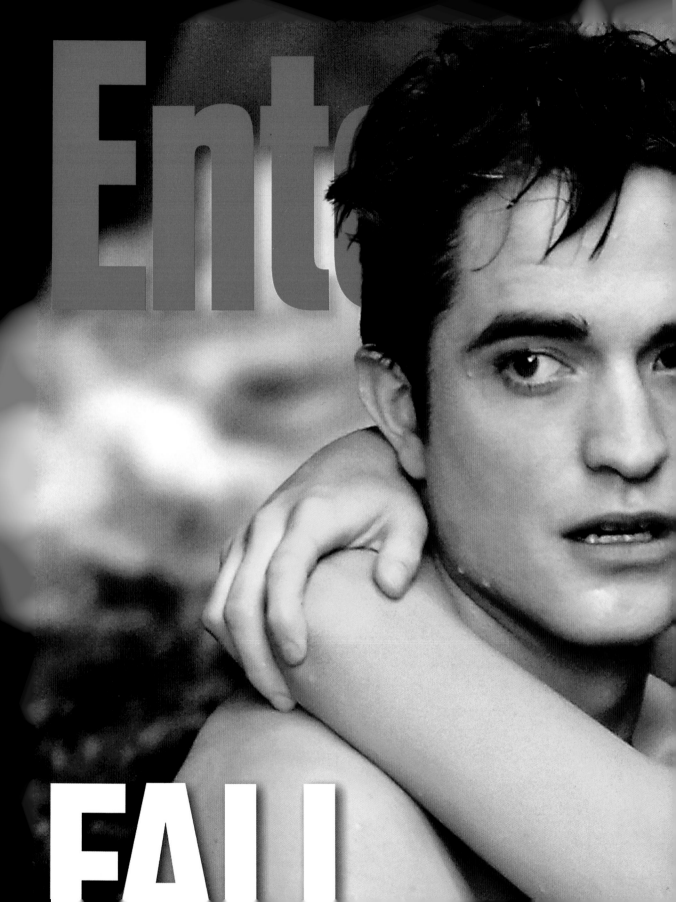

#1168/1169 • AUGUST 19/26, 2011

ment

WEEKLY

SPECIAL
DOUBLE
ISSUE

BY THE NUMBERS

ECLIPSE

2

Number of slightly bushier eyebrows Robert Pattinson sports after refusing to get them waxed like he did for the first movie

$300.5 MILLION

Total domestic gross

11⁴

Number of days *Eclipse* played in theaters

1

Number of early drafts of the screenplay that leaked on the Internet

4,000

Number of midnight showings on June 24, 2010

8

Number of deleted scenes on the two-disc special-edition DVD set

9.4 MILLION

Number of DVDs sold to date

58

Percentage of Fandango.com ticket buyers (based on a 1,000-customer sample) who said they were going to see the movie multiple times

$68 MILLION

Film's budget

45

Approximate miles per hour that vampires can run

193

Number of IMAX screens the movie opened on. (It was the first film of the series to play in IMAX.)

$698.5 MILLION

Total worldwide gross

Stewart
photographed for
EW by Sam Jones
on Nov. 4, 2011,
in Los Angeles

CHAPTER 4

THE LIGHT OF
DAWN

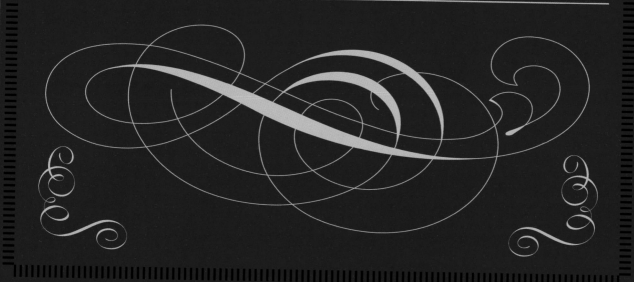

THE

HONEYM

Six months before **Breaking Dawn—Part 1** *hit theaters, we offered readers an exclusive sneak peek at the most controversial* Twilight *chapter yet, in which Bella conceives a half-human, half-vamp baby.*

BY **SARA VILKOMERSON**

THERE'S ONLY SO MUCH YOU CAN DO TO guard secrets on a set. When *Breaking Dawn* began shooting in November 2010, the filmmakers hired additional security and barred press from the set—all to keep audiences in a state of glorious suspense. But still, things happen. In March, grainy images—showing what appeared to be some of the more anticipated moments, including Bella and Edward in bed—leaked onto the Internet, prompting director Bill Condon and author Stephenie Meyer to request that fans avert their eyes. "It's hard not to feel that it was malicious in some way," says Condon. "It seemed like the very things we were most eager to keep a lid on were the ones that got exposed."

"It was gutting," adds Kristen Stewart. She figured the culprits had hacked into daily footage from the set, so she started leaving pointed messages at the end of her takes: "I'd be like, 'Hey, go for it! Just steal it, you f---ing a--holes!' They knew every moment that was important to people, and that's really what was so annoying."

You can't blame the cast and crew for getting especially riled up. *Breaking Dawn* wades into darker and murkier waters than the previous three installments in Meyer's *Twilight Saga*, and its 754 pages are rather eventful. Possibly inspired by that other frenzy-inducing franchise *Harry Potter*, Summit Entertainment decided to split *Breaking Dawn* into two movies that shot simultaneously for nearly six months at a punishing round-the-clock schedule on locations as far-flung as Baton Rouge, Vancouver, Rio de Janeiro, and the U.S. Virgin Islands.

The fact that the novel is so troubling and gothic could only have added to the strangeness of the enterprise. "When I read the book I asked myself, '*How* is this going to be a

Jacob

movie?'" says Taylor Lautner. "Everyone said it felt totally different than anything we've done before," says Stewart. "Just the fact that I'm sitting there pregnant—it's like, wow, are we really doing a *Twilight* movie?!" Pattinson, 24, agrees, fumbling for words to describe the plot: "There's just...it goes...there's definitely, um, some interesting and weird stuff going on."

This is, of course, the installment in which Bella and Edward marry and consummate their love amid flying feathers. Bella becomes pregnant with a half-vampire baby that grows inside her at an alarming rate, putting our heroine's life at grave risk, even as she endures a shockingly gruesome and violent labor. To prevent death from having the final word, Edward must turn Bella into a vampire. And that's just what happens in *Part 1*. "It is very much a departure," screenwriter Melissa Rosenberg says of the novel. "The first three books are about the love triangle. *Breaking Dawn* is really an adult story. I think the audience hopefully has grown up with the books and will appreciate it."

If they haven't matured with the books, they're about to grow up fast. "We shot everything—whether it's the lovemaking or the childbirth—as potent and powerful as it can be," says Condon, who nonetheless had to work within the constraints of PG-13. Stewart wishes the movie could have been even more graphic. "In some ways it was disappointing not to be able to really *go there*," she says. Asked if she ever imagined what an R-rated version of the film might look like, Stewart laughs and says, "We imagined it every single day."

It's not the honeymoon that Stewart wishes were more graphic ("It feels like a real love scene, not necessarily vampire-y, which is good") but the brutal birth of the baby, Renesmee. "It's funny because when [the PG-13 issue] comes up, everybody thinks it's all about the sex," she says. "The birth is really effective, and I've heard it really hits

OONERS

Edward and Bella
dive into marriage

you in the face. But what it *could* have been? It could have been shocking and grotesque, because that's how it was written in the book." She sighs: "I would have loved to have been puking up blood."

Bella's pregnancy is controversial for other reasons as well. Some readers have balked at what they interpreted to be a pro-life message in Meyer's novel, since Bella refuses to consider aborting her baby, even when she learns it could kill her. It was something the cast and crew had to come to terms with. Says Rosenberg, "It was an issue because I'm very pro-choice. But the truth is, *Twilight* is not the arena to be having the abortion debate. My approach to it is that having a child is a choice. More than a political issue, it's about Bella's reasoning, and articulating that was the challenge."

Stewart says she's in full agreement with her fictional counterpart: "I'm so on Bella's side. The idea of destroying something they made together that could never happen again… It has nothing to do with the pro-life thing. I just love the idea of her fighting. She's been willing to die for so much, but now you actually see her, well, *literally* die for it." The actress insists Bella's dilemma felt utterly real to her. "This really could happen to anyone my age. I mean, maybe not the whole vampire thing, but…I could f---ing get pregnant tomorrow."

AFTER SO MANY SCENES OF TERROR AND blood, the wedding sequence came as a relief. It was scheduled near the end of production and brought the cast together one final time, in Vancouver. "I never would have thought I'd be affected in this way, but it was one of the coolest things that I've done," says Stewart. "There was a certain point when I walked on set, and I saw everyone from the entire cast sitting there in the pews, about to do their bit. And it was just so perfect for me in that moment. It was so emotional in such a real way. I literally felt like thanking them for coming." Pattinson preferred filming the honeymoon in St. Thomas. "It was amazing finishing out in the Caribbean. It was like, why couldn't we have been shooting in the Caribbean the whole time? I would have done another five!"

The stars have clearly become close over the years, and not just Stewart and Pattinson. (They've actually never confirmed their relationship, but after those photos of them at the *Water for Elephants* premiere, they probably don't need to.) Pattinson, in a lovely bit of understatement, says this about his costars: "Having to spend so much time with people…it's just nice when you like them. There is a real bond. I think also there's something humbling about wearing the makeup and contacts." He laughs. "Except Taylor—he doesn't have to do a thing. He's managed [to do] no work on this last one. He's always a wolf!" Pattinson laughs again, anticipating *Breaking Dawn—Part 2*. "But he has to fall in love with a *baby*…. Oh, God, I can't wait to see how that goes."

When Lautner is told of Pattinson's ribbing, he says, "Oh my gosh. That sounds like him. Everybody is always complaining to me that I don't have to wear the contacts, I don't have to wear the white makeup or wear wigs. And I'm like, 'I'm the one in the freezing rain and cold not wearing a

Checkmate: the newlyweds on their honeymoon

"TAYLOR HAS TO FALL IN LOVE WITH A *BABY*," PATTINSON LAUGHS. "I CAN'T WAIT TO SEE HOW THAT GOES."

shirt! I paid my dues in *New Moon* and *Eclipse*.'" And as for imprinting on Renesmee? "There were many times I walked up to Stephenie [Meyer] and asked her, 'What exactly is imprinting?'" says Lautner. "It's still a very confusing thing for me, so don't ask."

"It's been quite a ride," he continues, on a more serious note. "It seems like just yesterday I was showing up to the set of *Twilight* and meeting the cast, and now here I am, years later, done filming. It's really the weirdest feeling."

Director Condon says he's looking forward to seeing where the actors' careers will take them. "Rob was the biggest surprise to me—just getting to know him," he says, noting that out of the three, Pattinson is the least like the character he plays. "You spend time with him and you think, 'God, I hope you get to play this incredibly smart, funny guy that you are.' Taylor is just a complete natural, a born entertainer. And Kristen," he laughs, "she's just hugely talented. I heard this great story about her that I think sums it up. She was pitched a female role in a comic-book superhero movie that's about to get started, and she was like, 'Well, screw that. I shouldn't be the superhero's girlfriend, I should be the superhero.' She's one of those people who will not fit into some kind of niche, but mold a career around who she is."

The actress, who started playing the part of Bella at 17 and celebrated her 21st birthday at the *Breaking Dawn* wrap party, agrees her real life has mingled with Bella's. "In the oddest ways, so many parallels can be drawn between my life and this series. Birthdays coincide, graduation, everything," she says. She's happy *Breaking Dawn* is over, she adds, but mostly because she knows they've done it right. "I really am so satisfied with the entire experience this time around," she says. "I really feel like we went through something, and it was captured. Who the f--- knows how it will turn out, but that's how it felt. We ended on such a high note, and that was the whole point of this one—to reach a state of exuberance."

Goodness, such positivity!

"I know, man, right?" Stewart laughs. "I'm so happy to be saying this to you, you have no idea." ◆

Edward and Bella

TO DIE FOR

*Pattinson, Stewart, and Lautner let loose on sex scenes,
birth scenes, and knocking costars unconscious.*

BY **SARA VILKOMERSON**

DUDE," SAYS KRISTEN Stewart. "There was something so sensory about it."

An hour ago Stewart, Taylor Lautner, and Robert Pattinson had their hand- and foot-prints immortalized in cement outside of Grauman's Chinese Theatre in Hollywood. Still giddy, palms stained a faint gray, the actress waxes poetic to her costars for a moment about how it felt when, right after leaving her prints for posterity, she impulsively grabbed Lautner's and Pattinson's hands. "The concrete was so gritty and I didn't even look, I just found your hands and it really felt like *something*," she says. The dudes she's speaking to, being dudes, promptly burst into laughter. Stewart glares at them with mock rage: "You know what? F--- you both right now *in the face* for laughing at me."

Pattinson smiles and teases her for how poised she was during the ceremony. "I noticed how slick you were," he says. "Everyone's always like, 'Kristen Stewart is so awkward.' And you're, like, Little Miss Slick nowadays."

It's not just Stewart who has grown up. *Breaking Dawn—Part 1* delves into some startling stuff: sex, pregnancy, and the horrific birth of a half-vampire baby. The trio—relentless in their affectionate teasing—talked to EW over coffee and pastries in Los Angeles.

Are you disappointed about anything that got trimmed in the movie?
TAYLOR LAUTNER The birth scene, for sure.
ROBERT PATTINSON Yes, the birth scene—and the sex scene.
KRISTEN STEWART Both. I wanted more from both of those.
PATTINSON Also, we've seen versions of those scenes that are *way* more—
STEWART Better.
I'm assuming the PG-13 rating was an issue.
PATTINSON It just limits things, like camera angles. Also there were these parts in the birth scene where Bella was in pain—
STEWART *That's* what I'm really disappointed about—and I've talked about it with Bill [Condon, the direc-tor]. It was more sympathetic or some-thing when I played the scene with less energy, and it made it easier for him to tell the story. But in the book, Bella is screaming, "NOOOOO!" [*Stewart stands and demonstrates.*] And I did it like that—crazy and *Exorcist*-like. I was going for this weird mix of turning into the most feral mother you can imagine and also fighting for my own life. I mean, I was a nutcase. I was an absolute nutcase.
PATTINSON Everyone was just s---ting themselves before we did [the birth scene] because it was such a big deal. But I think all three of us felt like it was a great day. To do a take that's five or six minutes long and feel like you've hit every beat...
LAUTNER I do still love the birth scene. I know it's frustrating that some things aren't in there.
STEWART Yeah, I still love it too.

Did you get to see any of the love-scene footage before it was sanitized?

PATTINSON There's a version where it was really intense.

STEWART In the book, you don't see the actual sex, but they talk about it afterwards and it's intense as hell. [Shooting the scene] wasn't a full experience because it was so fragmented. We did little individual shots of *his* face, *my* face, *his* hands. Cinematically, cut all together, it's awesome. I really like it, but we didn't really *do* that scene.

PATTINSON And when we did they kept telling us to stop. [*Laughs*]

STEWART I know! Bill kept going, "Stop thrusting" [*Laughs*].... I mean, I didn't want to *actually* have sex with him on set but...

PATTINSON Why not? [*Laughs*] You can see my butt crack—why does butt crack not make it an R? You see my butt crack the whole time.

STEWART No, you don't. They darkened it or something.

LAUTNER They shortened it, or I think they erased the crack.

PATTINSON It was really Kristen's fault it was going R-rated. [*To Stewart*] Your fancy moves—no one's seen moves like that in a PG-13 movie! [*Laughs*] The thing about ratings is, it's about noises.

STEWART Like if his thrust coincided with my *ohhhh*—that's not okay.

PATTINSON If a sex scene is rated R, the first thing you do is take out the sounds and put music over it. Same thing if there's a horror scene; you take out the screams.

LAUTNER Or in an action scene, if you're punching someone in the face you take out the sound effect of the fist making contact.

STEWART I punched Chris Hemsworth in the face last week [while shooting *Snow White and the Huntsman*]. Gave him a black eye.

LAUTNER What? For real? Were you supposed to?

STEWART I was supposed to miss him.

Have you ever given anyone a black eye before?

STEWART No. And I have to say for anyone who's ever been in that situation where, as a girl, you think it's not going to do anything—it f---ing does something.

LAUTNER [*Laughs*] Wow.

"I DID IT *EXORCIST*-LIKE," STEWART SAYS OF A MORE INTENSE VERSION OF THE BIRTH SCENE. "I WAS AN ABSOLUTE NUTCASE."

STEWART Yup! He was standing over me, like, Huntsman-ing out, and I just went *boom*. I spun him around. I punched him right out of his close-up! And then I started crying. I felt horrible.

LAUTNER Are you kidding me? I know you feel horrible in the moment, but afterwards did you feel kind of good?

STEWART It felt good in the way, like, I know this [*gestures to her fist*] works now. I can punch Chris Hemsworth. I can spin that man around! And I didn't do it as hard as I could.

LAUTNER I did the same thing on *Abduction*.

STEWART You hit someone?

LAUTNER Yeah. He went out, though. [*To Pattinson*] It was actually the guy that played your father in *Water for Elephants*.

PATTINSON Oh my God!

STEWART You knocked him unconscious?

LAUTNER Yes! And he's *huge*. It was just for a split second. He came to right away.

Rob, how about you? Have you ever knocked anyone out on film?

PATTINSON I think I punched someone in the face in *Remember Me*. There was this bit where I was on the floor hitting someone repeatedly, and I kept being like, [*whispers*] "Sorry, sorry." But he didn't seem to feel it at all. [*Laughter*]

Rob, the last time we talked you called Edward a "pussy," in part because he carries a bucket around for Bella to vomit in when she's pregnant and sick. I thought you were just being metaphorical. Then I saw the movie, and you actually do hold a bucket for Bella when she's sick.

STEWART And that's *not* pussy behavior, in my opinion.

PATTINSON That wasn't the pussy part of it. The pussy part of it was the other stuff. The pussy part...

LAUTNER Just say it! [*Laughs*]

STEWART Dude! No more! Do not say "pussy part" again. This is very typical of a conversation we would have on the set.

PATTINSON [*Making fun of himself*] "I don't understand, Bill! What is this? I'm going to leave the set if you make me do this *pussy part* behavior..."

STEWART The thing is, we're joking now. This is all in jest. But on set this always went on! [*Gestures to Pattinson*] I could *kill* him sometimes. [*Looks affectionately at Pattinson, who just finished eating a piece of pastry*] You've got s--- all over your face. You look like a fool.

So now that you've moved on to different projects, does it feel like starting at a new school?

STEWART It's like that all the time. That's what being in this business feels like.

Bella feels the first signs of motherhood as Edward looks on

#1182
NOV. 25, 2011

Enterta

**BREAKING
DAWN**

LAUTNER That's the normal thing. *Twilight* is the unnormal.

PATTINSON Also, because of the *Twilight* fame, you arrive on a set with a certain familiarity anyway. People will treat you differently.

STEWART [*Sighs*] Yeah, it's weird. It's the strangest part of being "famous" because you don't get to give first impressions anymore. Everyone already has an impression of you before you meet them.

PATTINSON So you feel like you're already defending yourself. Also you need to become fast friends with people on a movie, especially the cast, and if you can't go out with people or socialize with them in a real way...

STEWART It's harmful.

Would any of you ever do TV?

PATTINSON I would, yeah. I've never been as invested as I was with *The Wire*. I've never met anyone from *The Wire* and I think if I ever saw anyone—Michael K. Williams or David Simon—I would literally cry. I would play every part in *The Wire* if they ever did another series.

STEWART I wouldn't want to. When I start production on a film—and I know I've used this metaphor a million times—but it's like I'm a shook-up can of Coke. All I want is to be done, as much as I love the process.

Does producing or directing interest you?

STEWART Right now on *Snow White*, I'm having the most fulfilling experience as an actor. I'm close with the director [Rupert Sanders], have his ear, and it's to his credit that I feel this way because I'm getting my first taste of really collaborating. Usually as an actor you put your hands up and go, "That's not my thing." And I love acting. But it's also so cool to be on their level, to give an opinion and be taken seriously.

So what do you want to do next?

STEWART I want to go home. I can't wait to not be working and go home and gain some interests. [*Laughs*] I want to see what I'm into. I want to figure out what I want. I can't answer this question right now, but I can't wait to be able to.

Taylor, there have been reports that you and Gus Van Sant are teaming for a movie based on an article in *The New Yorker* that you acquired.

LAUTNER It's extremely premature. I love Gus and have always been a huge fan of his. I never thought I'd have an opportunity to work with him, so...we'll see.

So what are we allowed to know?

LAUTNER That I'm a huge Gus Van Sant fan. [*Laughs*]

PATTINSON But now I want to know what it is.

Is it hard when your other films, like *Abduction* or *Water for Elephants*, don't perform at the box office like a *Twilight* movie?

STEWART You can't ever compare.

LAUTNER You just have to tell yourself *this* is otherworldly. You've got to know that going in.

PATTINSON There are two ways to go about it.... I mean, there's no way to have your movies be massively successful and get 100 percent of the critical praise every single time.

LAUTNER Right.

PATTINSON It's impossible. If you're trying to sell a movie or a project to a studio and you imply for one second that you're an artist, you're out the door.

There are actors who seem to be able to do both indie films and big studio films.

PATTINSON But how many people are there, really, who can do that?

STEWART Dude! So you don't think they exist? There are phenomenal actors that do big commercial movies and small ones. Catherine Keener! Julianne Moore! There are lots.

PATTINSON Look at you, just waiting to contradict me.

STEWART It's just that this is what I want to *be*. So if you say it doesn't exist, that's big for me! Like, that's all I aspire to and you are saying it doesn't exist. You *don't* have to choose one road or another.

There are definitely actors who can do both.

STEWART Right? [*She grins, putting a hand on both Pattinson's and Lautner's knees.*] C'mon, guys! Let's see if we can do this. ◆

ON THE SET

To shoot the **Breaking Dawn** *movies,*
the Twilight *clan traveled all over the globe*

"It was completely mixed up," says Pattinson
of shooting both *Breaking Dawn* films
simultaneously. "We did quite a few days
when we did one movie in the morning and the
second in the afternoon." (Clockwise from top)
Director Bill Condon talks Stewart and Pattinson
through Bella and Edward's much-anticipated
consummation scene in Baton Rouge, La.;
Stewart comes up for air on location in Brazil;
Stewart prepares to be the blushing bride
on set in Canada; Pattinson and Stewart film
the speedboat scene in Brazil.

BREAKING DAWN—PART 1 PREMIERES
FAN FRENZY!

(Above) Pattinson, Stewart, and Lautner present a united front at the *Breaking Dawn—Part 1* premiere on Nov. 14, 2011, at the Nokia Theatre in Los Angeles; (below) fans scream their devotion to the cast.

We flew 3,700 mile

BY THE NUMBERS

BREAKING DAWN—PART 1

$25 MILLION

Reported amount that Stewart, Pattinson, and Lautner were each paid for both *Breaking Dawn* movies

80

Percentage of *Breaking Dawn*'s opening-weekend audience that was female

$2,999.99

Price of pillow from Edward and Bella's love scene, sold on eBay.com

$110 MILLION

Film's budget

$281.2 MILLION

Total domestic gross

5.2 MILLION

Number of DVDs sold to date

$35,000

Estimated cost of Bella's wedding dress

2

Number of men who reported suffering seizures after watching the birth scene

$29.99

Price of a pair of red contact lenses similar to those worn by *Twilight* actors playing vampires

$705.1 MILLION

Total worldwide gross

Stewart, Mackenzie
Foy, and Pattinson

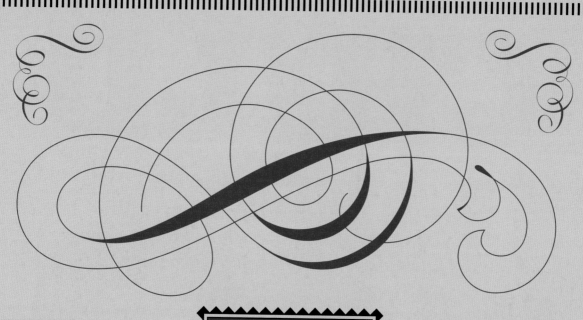

CHAPTER 5

THE TWILIGHT FINALE

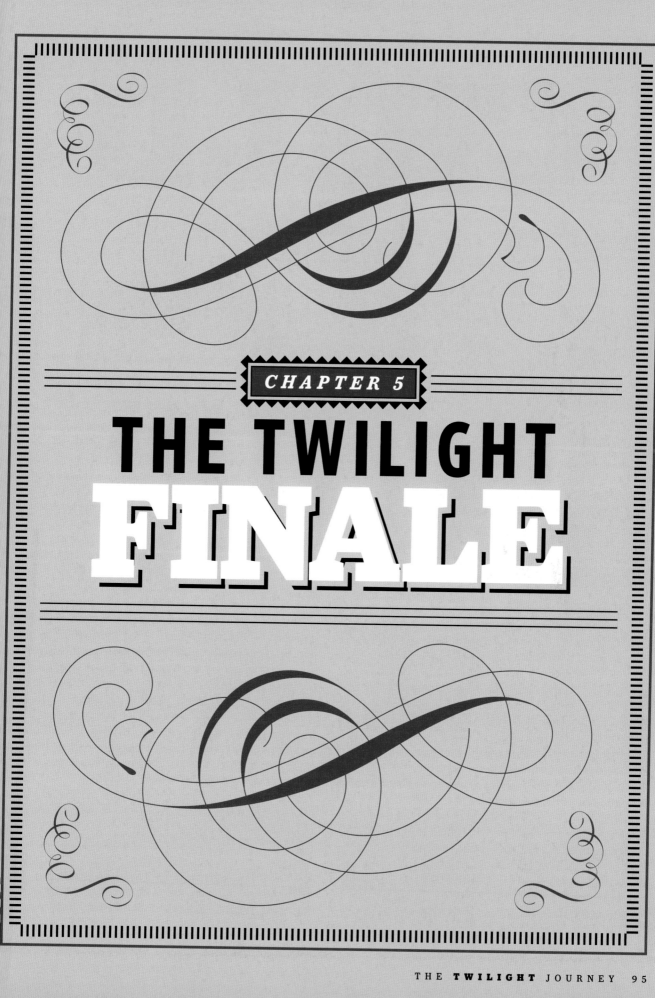

SWEET
CHILD
O'MINE

Our first story on the very last Twilight *movie,*
Breaking Dawn—Part 2, *gave readers an exclusive glimpse of Edward and Bella's daughter, Renesmee.*

BY **SARA VILKOMERSON**

HOW TO EXPLAIN *THE TWILIGHT Saga: Breaking Dawn—Part 2?* Let's hear Robert Pattinson give it a shot. The actor, 26, says this final installment of the franchise is "stranger than all the other films put together." He pauses. He sighs. He stammers (charmingly, British-ly) before arriving at a surprisingly simple resting place: "Vampires are weird."

And getting weirder all the time. Pattinson's larger point is that while the previous *Twilight* movies have always kept one foot in reality (girl-meets-vampire reality, anyway), Stephenie Meyer's *Breaking Dawn* is a 754-page tonal departure, so packed with plot twists and new characters that Summit Entertainment split it into two films. But considering that *Part 1* ended with Bella dying—and coming back to sorta life by opening her glowing, telltale-red vampiric eyes, fans knew things were just getting started. What you will see in these pages is an exclusive first look at Bella and Edward's daughter, Renesmee (Mackenzie Foy, 11), the halfling child over whom all manner of hell will break loose.

"Let me tell you, this movie is *so* weird," confirms Kristen Stewart, 22, clearly intending this as a compliment. "It. Is. Bizarre." Bill Condon, who directed both installments of *Breaking Dawn* from scripts by Melissa Rosenberg, says he was excited by how different the two movies would be. "I always thought of *Part 1* as having two distinct halves: the romantic and the horror," he says. "But this one is epic. This is a whole different thing."

Let's begin with one of the more obvious differences between *Breaking Dawn—Part 2* and all that came before. Bella has now left the mortal world behind and joined the sparkly-skinned Cullen clan both physically and spiritually. Says Taylor Lautner, 20, "That's kind of the huge thing that fans are waiting for—to see the clumsy teenage Bella that Kristen did so well suddenly become this supersexy vampire who's athletic and graceful. She took it very seriously and pulls it off." Condon agrees: "I don't think you can grasp how major an achievement it is till you see it. Her transformation from high school girl to fierce warrior is amazing. She's a different species now." Stewart says that years of watching her castmates helped inform how she played Vampire Bella. "I know every single version of vampire, and I took a little bit from everyone," she says with a laugh. "But I wanted her to be the best one."

Not that it didn't take some adjusting. "Kristen complained about 500 times more than I have," says Pattinson of the uncomfortable red contact lenses that the actors playing vampires must wear. "She condensed four years of complaining into a few months." (Stewart, long used to Pattinson's teasing ways, sighs in response to this and reminds EW that she's been wearing brown contact lenses over her green eyes since the series began.) Performing in high heels during action-heavy scenes did not come easily—Stewart jokes that the kind of preternatural grace Bella possesses as a vampire "does not actually exist" in the actress playing her—but she did manage to locate her inner bloodsucker while shooting a scene in which Bella hunts a mountain lion. "I leaped through the air and tackled a crazy huge tube of foam shaped like a mountain lion," she says. "I ripped that mother to *the ground*! For the first time I was like, 'Wow, I'm, like, *really* playing a vampire now.'"

One source of Bella's newfound ferocity is her daughter, Renesmee, the half-human, half-vampire baby maturing at an unnatural rate, lies at the heart of the drama in *Part 2*. The vampire ruling class known as the Volturi mistakenly believe

Bella and Renesmee (Foy) spend an emotional night together on the eve of their final confrontation with the Volturi

"LET ME TELL YOU," SAYS STEWART, "THIS MOVIE IS *SO* WEIRD. IT. IS. BIZARRE."

Vampire covens convene

that Renesmee is a human youngster turned into a vampire, which is a serious no-no in Meyer's bloodsucker world, so they intend to snuff out the Cullens as punishment. (The girl has some decidedly vamp qualities but is also very much human, heartbeat and all.) Condon spotted Foy early in the audition process. "It's a hugely important part," he says. "There were a lot of kids. But this was kind of obvious. It was one of those rare times when you see something—like with an apartment or house—and it feels good and you just need to take it. I felt that way, like, '*Oh, this is good.*'" Foy seems remarkably unfazed by the time spent with her überfamous costars. "They are supernice," she says.

Condon says it went well beyond superficialities. "They were *amazing* with her," he says. "It really brought something paternal out in Rob, and Kristen was especially protective. I'd have to interrupt them when they were in deep conversation to get going with a scene." It helped that Stewart began her own acting career as a child, in movies such as *The Safety of Objects* and *Panic Room*. "I loved chatting with Mackenzie," she says. "I'm always curious about what's going on in the minds of kids on set. She's really close to the age I was when I started."

Pattinson points out that having an impressionable youth on the set curbed certain cast members' predilection for raucousness. "We're all around the same age and we're really not polite to each other anymore. You'd have to tone it down when Mackenzie was around," he says. Or at least attempt to. "She had a little swear jar, and I think she made 850 bucks or something." (Stewart, known to work blue in casual speech, laughs when asked if she managed to respect the swear jar: "Uh, yeah, no.")

P LAYING A MOTHER TO AN 11-YEAR-OLD actress, Stewart says, might have been difficult in a more traditional context, but this being the Twili-verse, it was easier to wrap her head around mothering a child who in real life is only a decade or so younger: "[My relationship with Renesmee] is so completely rooted in this world, and I could relate to it because I very much believe it." Bella and Renesmee's bond is a particularly special one, complete with supernatural methods of communication. "It's a really cool relationship. I hope it comes across," Stewart says. And having an actress like Foy, who (rather spookily) resembles both her and Pattinson, didn't hurt either. "Even our hands look similar," Stewart says. "It was kind of strange. But it's funny how it actually helps. It's like, 'Oh, hey, you look like me, kid! Come on!'"

Renesmee, of course, has a supernatural link to a certain older man as well. Jacob, who's spent most of the series in

Bella and dad Charlie embrace

"FOR THE FIRST TIME I WAS LIKE, 'WOW, I'M, LIKE, *REALLY* PLAYING A VAMPIRE NOW,'" SAYS STEWART.

unrequited love with Bella, has imprinted on the infant Renesmee—"imprinting" being the process by which his tribe of werewolves suddenly discover who their soul mates are. In the past, Lautner has said he found the metaphysical mechanics of it all a bit confusing. But talking to Stephenie Meyer and diving back into the book got him more comfortable with the notion of being in love with a child. "Everyone likes to tease me about it," he says. "Everyone thinks it's so funny, and I laugh along with them, but it's important for me to keep in my mind that it's as simple as a lifelong bond. It's not nearly as creepy as everybody likes to joke." That "everybody" includes Pattinson, needless to say. "Oh, I can't wait till he has to do live TV," Pattinson says of Lautner with a gleeful cackle. "Did you ask him if his taste in women has changed? The first scene I saw them together, I literally could not stop laughing. I wouldn't have been able to do it." Lautner remains resolute: "I think people will be very happy with the whole imprinting situation."

Joking aside, imprinting provides an elegant solution to the love triangle that's fueled years of Team Edward/ Team Jacob rivalries. Once Jacob's heart is promised to Renesmee, the three principal characters find themselves on the same side against a common enemy. It offered Lautner an opportunity to act beyond the part of despondent suitor. "For me *Part 2* is so great because it's a completely different side of Jacob that we've never seen before," he says. "He's always had one goal: to be with Bella. In this one, he's happy! He's much more relaxed and comedic. The trio was so tense and the triangle is still here, but it's a completely different relationship between them."

Breaking Dawn—Part 2's conclusion revolves around a confrontation on a field between a multitude of Volturi and the Cullen clan, who have rallied friends from all over the globe for backup. Translation: An awful lot of new vampire characters were on set, along with tons of extras.

For Condon, it was a challenge logistically—and not just because it took about an hour to get everyone through the lunch line. "The first part of *Breaking Dawn* was all about these crucial moments: wedding, pregnancy, birth, and death. There was a clear path. Here we introduce 23 new vampires and have hundreds of extra Volturi, so it was just about making sure that we had the same kind of clarity." The director had never filmed an epic battle scene before, but his résumé (which includes *Dreamgirls*) wound up serving him well. "Ultimately you treat it like a musical," he says. "It's all about a rhythm."

Maybe, but filming the climax was still a nightmare, according to his cast. "Everyone started to go absolutely

KNOW YOUR VAMPIRES

Let's compare bloodsuckers from all walks of pop culture

	Sleep in coffins	Repelled by garlic	Affected by sunlight	Retractable fangs	Obsessed with counting
TWILIGHT	NO	NO	☀	NO	NO
INTERVIEW WITH THE VAMPIRE	⚰	🧄	☀	NO	NO
BRAM STOKER'S DRACULA	⚰	🧄	☀	🦷	NO
BUFFY THE VAMPIRE SLAYER	NO	🧄	☀	🦷	NO
BLADE	⚰	🧄	☀	🦷	NO
LET THE RIGHT ONE IN	NO	NO	☀	NO	NO
TRUE BLOOD	⚰	NO	☀	🦷	NO
THE VAMPIRE DIARIES	NO	NO	☀	🦷	NO
UNDERWORLD SERIES	⚰	NO	☀	🦷	NO
COUNT VON COUNT	NO	NO	NO	NO	1

Vampire Bella

"JACOB'S ALWAYS HAD ONE GOAL: TO BE WITH BELLA. BUT IN THIS ONE, HE'S HAPPY!" SAYS LAUTNER.

insane," says Stewart with a laugh. "It moves so quickly in the movie, but it took so long to film. There was so much dialogue and so much to shoot and so many people and so many story lines." Much of the action took place in a warehouse, and shooting this particular sequence dragged out over a couple of months, including additional reshoots for a few of the principals. "Oh, gosh, we spent my life on that field with the fake snow and the greenscreen," says Stewart. "[The fake snow] gets under your contacts and into your lungs. It's horrible s---. It's the end of our movie, and it's a big deal to really bring it to the high point it deserves. But yeah, it was a mind-losing experience."

Team *Twilight* says that the resulting scenes were worth the effort, and we'll take them at their word. They also say there's some kind of visual valentine to fans in the closing moments. Pattinson, who's seen a rough cut of the film, found himself surprisingly moved. "The end is so sweet. There's this nice finality to it," he says. "Everyone who was watching started crying. It does a serious justice to the series."

Stewart emphatically agrees. "Bill decided to do this really f---ing amazing thing at the very end," she says. "The fans are going to go nuts." No doubt. Pandemonium is coming soon to a theater near you. ◆

Bella and Edward

SURVIVING A
SCANDAL

Fans reeled when Stewart admitted to straying, but Breaking Dawn *director Bill Condon urged them to remember she'd always been loyal to* them.

BY **SARA VILKOMERSON**

FOREVER—THE WORD AND THE concept—is a Very Big Deal within the *Twilight* universe. "Forever" is the tagline on the early posters for *Breaking Dawn— Part 2*, as well as the goal for the final installment of the blockbuster franchise: an eternal happily-ever-after for Bella, Edward, and Jacob. Moviegoers who've followed the trio with intense devotion since the first film opened in 2008 want and expect nothing less.

In real life, though, *forever* can be more elusive. When photographs of Kristen Stewart, 22, kissing her married *Snow White and the Huntsman* director, Rupert

Sanders, 41, surfaced on July 24, they whipped the media into an almost hysterical lather. The actress issued an immediate public apology, directed to her never-before-confirmed live-in boyfriend, Robert Pattinson, 26: "This momentary indiscretion has jeopardized the most important thing in my life, the person I love and respect the most, Rob. I love him, I love him, I'm so sorry." That only managed to increase the furor.

Let's just say people took the news rather personally. London's *The Sun* declared Stewart the most hated woman in Hollywood. Apoplectic fans flooded YouTube with outraged videos. New York's *Daily News* labeled her a "trampire." That so much vitriol is being heaped upon a young, unmarried woman is both disheartening and unfair

MACKENZIE FOY

JOINS THE CAST

AGE 11
HOMETOWN Los Angeles

FIRST JOB Modeling for Ralph Lauren at the age of 3. She's since worked steadily—modeling, appearing in commercials, and acting on TV shows such as *'Til Death*, *Hawaii Five-0*, and *FlashForward*.

BABE IN THE WOODS Just because Foy has a major role in *Breaking Dawn—Part 2* doesn't mean she's allowed to watch all the *Twilight* movies. "I've seen the first one and the second one, but I'm not allowed to watch the third one." She does, however, think she will be able to see at least some of her scenes in *Part 2*.

TWI-ING NEW THINGS During shooting, Foy picked up some skills from her famous costars. Lautner taught her how to throw a football, and Stewart gave her tips on summoning tears: "She said to think of something sad for a very long time."

SUMMER BREAK The actress, who is homeschooled, just completed fifth grade. She says without hesitation that she'd like to act for the rest of her life—as well as direct. In the near future? "Nothing. I'm going to swim and eat Popsicles."

(do *you* remember making any poor choices at 22?). But it underscores how blurry the line is between *Twilight*'s fiction and these young actors' reality.

For better or worse, Stewart and Pattinson and their much-speculated-upon romance have always been intertwined with the onscreen relationship of their fictional counterparts, Bella and Edward. In *Breaking Dawn—Part 2*, newlywed Bella is finally a vampire and can spend eternity in love with her husband. No one can know what will happen in the private lives of Pattinson and Stewart, who are very much human.

"The fact is, these are actors playing parts," says Bill Condon, director of *Breaking Dawn—Part 1* and *2*. "Maybe it's not such a bad thing for people to be reminded of that." Condon, who says he has not spoken to either of his young stars since the story broke in July, understandably wants fans to watch his movie without letting messy real life get in the way. "Both of these actors gave heart and soul to the *Twilight* movies, not only during shooting, but also by navigating so graciously the whole life-in-a-fishbowl aspect of the

phenomenon," he says. "Above all, they have always shown great respect for the fans who made these movies such a success. Now it's time that some of that respect be returned to them."

ABOUT A WEEK AND A half before the Twili-verse imploded, EW sat down with Stewart, Pattinson, and Taylor Lautner on a sunny San Diego afternoon. Nothing seemed amiss. In fact, the trio were particularly relaxed after enduring their final Comic-Con press conference. Lautner, 20, stretched out in an armchair. Stewart kicked off her shoes and curled up on a sofa beside Pattinson, occasionally leaning over to nudge him when his attention waned or his answers meandered.

Not that you can blame him. *Breaking Dawn—Part 2*, which Pattinson calls "stranger than all the other films put together," is indeed a hard film to explain. *Part 1* was all about Bella's wedding, her honeymoon, her pregnancy, and the violent birth of a baby girl who technically kills her but also allows her to return as a full-fledged member of the Cullen vampire clan.

Jacob and Renesmee

Emmett and Bella test their vampire strength

Part 2 ventures even further from reality, with just about everyone in the film (except for Bella's father, Charlie) either a vampire or a member of Jacob's wolf pack. Accordingly, there's a lot more action. "The second film takes place right where the first one ends, but it's almost like they're in different genres," says Condon, who shot the films simultaneously.

Playing a vampire instead of an awkward high schooler, Stewart digs into her role with claws and teeth. She ferociously stalks prey in the forest—the Comic-Con crowd cheered at footage of her taking down a mountain lion—and appears taller, sexier, and somehow much more dangerous on screen. Meanwhile, Jacob, who has spent so much of the series pining for Bella, finds true love after "imprinting" on Bella and Edward's infant child, Renesmee (played by 11-year-old newcomer Mackenzie Foy). As if all this weren't complicated enough, the real drama of *Part 2* comes courtesy of an unfortunate miscommunication with the ruling vampire class known as the Volturi, who mistakenly believe that Renesmee was born human and then turned. (Vampire babies are a violation of vampire law, the punishment being death for both the child and the makers.) Of course, Renesmee *is* half human, growing toward adulthood at a preternatural rate. So the Cullens assemble an international vampire alliance to testify that Renesmee grows and ages.

Got all that? Well, just you wait: Even devoted readers of the Stephenie Meyer books are in for a pretty big shock in the final third of the film, when the plot strays from the last novel in a sequence dreamed up by Meyer and long-time screenwriter Melissa Rosenberg one night over dinner. "When I first read the script, I got to that part and was like, '*What?*'" Pattinson says. "And then I had to go back a page."

The actors stress that they hope the film's surprises won't leak out—so we won't spoil anything here. But we *can* tell you that even those averse to change will be more than satisfied, and probably thrilled, by how the series ends. The actors certainly are. "It's clearly made by someone who really likes [the saga], who really cares," Stewart says. "That's why Bill Condon is perfect. Thank God for him."

Still, getting there wasn't always smooth. Shooting the two films back-to-back took almost six months—with plenty of complaining along the way. ("It's a really easy way to cause dissent within a cast—stick contact lenses on them," says Pattinson of the obligatory golden vampire eyes.) For Condon, one of the biggest challenges was depicting Renesmee's rapid rate of growth. Nearly a dozen girls of different ages stood in for Renesmee during

"BOTH KRISTEN AND ROB GAVE THEIR HEART AND SOUL TO THE *TWILIGHT* MOVIES," SAYS CONDON.

production, and Foy's face was digitally added later, via F/X, as with *The Curious Case of Benjamin Button.*

But before stumbling on that CG-based approach, Condon commissioned a nearly three-foot-tall Renesmee doll ("that robot-baby," as Pattinson calls it), which was quickly deemed an epic fail. "Did you see it? That *thiiing*," Lautner says, joining Stewart and Pattinson in giggles. The ill-fated prop even got its own name: Chuckesmee. "Chuckesmee was a giant misfire on all fronts," Condon concedes. "Truly, it was one of the most grotesque things I've ever seen. It was a horror show! There was one shot where I call, 'Cut,' and suddenly she turns her head and mechanically stares right into the camera. It was incredibly disturbing." (Condon promises that Chuckesmee, who never turns up in the finished film, will appear on the DVD extras.)

YOUR WHOLE LIFE IS BECOMING PART OF the performance," Pattinson said back in July. "People watch a character through a prism of how they perceive you in public."

Those public perceptions are taking a beating in light of recent developments, creating a new challenge for Summit Entertainment, the studio releasing the film, as it gears up to promote the final *Twilight* installment. "While it is studio policy not to comment on the personal lives of actors, Summit is moving full steam ahead," Nancy Kirkpatrick, the company's head of worldwide marketing, told EW. But questions linger: What happens during an international press tour and red-carpet premiere when the two top-billed stars may or may not be speaking to each other? Will the news change how the

"I'VE NEVER BEEN ABLE TO FORM THIS *PERSONA* THAT SOME PEOPLE ARE SO GOOD AT," SAYS STEWART.

Edward and Bella

film plays for Twihards? And what effect will any of this have on Pattinson's and Stewart's future projects?

It's tempting to attach greater meaning to comments the *Twilight* stars made in a more innocent time, just a few weeks ago. But the truth is that even in San Diego, the actors were already feeling somewhat reflective as their five-year journey was reaching an end, clearly coming to terms with the many ways the franchise has changed them. What life lessons had they learned from their characters? EW wondered. Lautner answered first. "I respect how passionate and persistent Jacob is about what he loves and what he wants. He's not going to let anything stop him from that. That's the thing that's stuck with me."

Pattinson marveled at Edward's unflappable ability to stay rational. "It's strange. All through the series, it's like, 'Hey, this guy is trying to be sensible! Let's think this thing out.' And everyone is like, 'F--- you!' " he said with a laugh. "But

what did you learn?" prodded Stewart. Pattinson answered, still laughing, "Don't be pragmatic. Be an emotional idiot."

Then Stewart chimed in about her ongoing struggle to carve out a public life that feels authentic. "I've never been able to fully form this thing, this *persona*, that some people are so f---ing good at. That's an art. I know a lot of actors [who can do that], and you guys aren't them," she said, gesturing to Lautner and Pattinson.

"Did you just point to us?" Pattinson asked.

"Yeah," Stewart said. "And *thank God*! I don't like people like that. People who are a complete nonperson but somehow through the lens seem like they are *on* and interesting and engaged. I care way more about the people standing in the room. I don't want anyone leaving and saying, 'God, that girl is so fake.' People tell me to make it easier on myself and to play a character when I go out on carpets and stuff," she said. "But you know what? I'd rather be me." ◆

THE LAST
WORD

Stephenie Meyer says she misses the cast already. The Twilight *author looks back on the movies.*

BY **SARA VILKOMERSON**

STEPHENIE MEYER'S *Twilight Saga* has sold more than 100 million books, spawning a film franchise that's become an international sensation. When EW met with the author, 38, at Comic-Con in July, she was already at work on two more adaptations, of her own 2008 novel *The Host* (in theaters March 29, 2013) and Lois Duncan's 1974 young-adult classic *Down a Dark Hall*.

Meyer on the *Breaking Dawn—Part 2* **set**

After *Breaking Dawn—Part 2*, **we'll have reached the cinematic end of** *The Twilight Saga*. **How are you feeling?**
I've been holding off the sadness, but it's starting to get to me. I miss everyone—Kristen, Taylor, and Rob. I'm used to seeing them every day.

You're currently working on a film adaptation of another of your books, *The Host*. **Has your experience with** *Twilight* **changed how you feel about turning your books into movies?**
It's hard to say. As a general rule, my experience has been positive, and as an author I don't think anyone has been offered the access I've had. With every movie I've become a little bit more involved. I really like to be used as a resource—like if an actor has a question about backstory. And recently, on the set of *The Host*, I was the only person on the entire set who noticed that there was a cherry-picker tractor in the back of a scene. So I'm useful every now and then—I have fantastic eyesight. [*Laughs*]

You even had a cameo in *Breaking Dawn—Part 1*, **as a wedding guest at Edward and Bella's wedding.**
It wasn't my idea—and I hated that dress! I hate to look at myself on film. But the actual experience, aside from freezing our butts off, was great. I was sitting with [producer] Wyck Godfrey, who has also been there since day one, and we made up a backstory: He was a deputy policeman, and our marriage was on the rocks because he was in love with [Bella's father] Charlie. We had a lot of fun sitting in that cold forest.

You named Bella and Edward's daughter Renesmee, which has been a source of ridicule even among ardent *Twilight* **fans.**
I am someone who strongly believes in reality, and that you don't monkey around with people's names. Whether they become a stripper or a lawyer has a large part to do with the name you give them. I would never name a real child Renesmee. But in fantasy, you can name your characters anything you want. I couldn't have named [Bella and Edward's] child Lindsay. I couldn't have named her anything that already exists—it would have felt wrong. I had to pick a name that I felt was completely and totally unique, which opens you up to heckling. Which I've taken. I take all my heckling, and I totally get it!

Someone is probably naming their real-life child Renesmee even as we speak.
Well, that really disturbs me. [*Laughs*]

Do you have a favorite among the *Twilight* **movies?**
Not to say it's the best, because all of them have things to recommend them, but I think *New Moon* is the one that most closely dovetails with what I had in my head. It might help that I love [director] Chris Weitz—he's a dream to work with. Everyone was fun to work with, but Chris and I really got each other.

When you were writing the first *Twilight*, **could you ever have imagined it would become such a huge phenomenon?**
If I'd had any idea that anyone would see what I was doing, I'd have stopped immediately. I'd never have been able to finish it. It's a huge amount of pressure, and it's taken me forever to be able to call myself an author. I'm a *reader*, and to me authors are magical creatures.

Do you ever watch *True Blood* **or** *The Vampire Diaries* **to see what all these other vampires are up to?**
No. I'm a huge coward. [*Laughs*] I'm actually really squeamish. ◆

Pattinson
photographed fo
EW by Ben Watts
on Oct. 12, 2009,
in Vancouver

Stewart and Lautner
photographed for EW
by Ben Watts
on June 3, 2009,
in Agoura, Calif.

Pattinson and Stewart
photographed for EW by
Jeff Riedel on June 6,
2008, in Los Angeles

Pattinson and Stewart
photographed for EW by
James White on Sept. 16,
2008, in Los Angeles

OCT 1 5 2012
$17.95